T0339543

Migration Law and the Externalization of Border Controls

Over the last few decades, both the European Union and European States have been implementing various strategies to externalize border controls with the declared intent of saving human lives and countering smuggling but with the actual end result of shifting borders, circumventing international obligations and ultimately preventing access to Europe. What has been principally deplored is the fact that externalizing border controls risks creating 'legal black holes'. Furthermore, what is particularly worrying in the current European debate is the intensification of this practice by multiple arrangements with unsafe third countries, exposing migrants and asylum seekers to serious human rights violations.

This book explores whether European States can succeed in shifting their responsibility onto Third States in cases of human rights violations. Focusing, in particular, on the 2017 Italy-Libya Memorandum of Understanding, the book investigates the possible basis for triggering the responsibility of outsourcing States. The second part of the book examines how the Italy-Libya MoU is only a small part of a broader scenario, exploring EU policies of externalization. A brief overview of the recent decisions of the EU Court vis-à-vis two aspects of externalization (the EU-Turkey statement and the issue of humanitarian visas) will pave the way for the conclusions since, in the author's view, the current attitude of the Luxembourg Court confirms the importance of focusing on the responsibility of European States and the urgent need to investigate the possibility of bringing a claim against the outsourcing States before the Court of Strasbourg.

Offering a new perspective on an extremely topical subject, this book will appeal to students, scholars and practitioners with an interest in European Law, International Law, Migration and Human Rights.

Anna Liguori is Associate Professor of International Law at "L'Orientale" University of Naples, Italy.

Routledge Research in EU Law

https://www.routledge.com/Routledge-Research-in-EU-Law/book-series/
ROUTEULAW

Migration Law and the Externalization of Border Controls

European State Responsibility

Anna Liguori

Routledge
Taylor & Francis Group

LONDON AND NEW YORK

First published 2019
by Routledge
2 Park Square, Milton Park, Abingdon, Oxon OX14 4RN

and by Routledge
605 Third Avenue, New York, NY 10017

First issued in paperback 2021

Routledge is an imprint of the Taylor & Francis Group, an informa business

Publisher's Note
The publisher has gone to great lengths to ensure the quality of this reprint but points out that some imperfections in the original copies may be apparent.

British Library Cataloguing-in-Publication Data
A catalogue record for this book is available from the British Library

Library of Congress Cataloging-in-Publication Data
Names: Liguori, Anna, author.
Title: Migration law and the externalization of border controls: European state responsibility / Anna Liguori.
Description: New York: Routledge, 2019. |
Series: Routledge research in eu law |
Includes bibliographical references and index.
Identifiers: LCCN 2018060411 (print) | LCCN 2018060626 (ebook) |
ISBN 9780429439100 (ebk) | ISBN 9781138343481 (hbk)
Subjects: LCSH: Emigration and immigration law—European Union countries. | Immigrants—Civil rights—European Union countries. | Immigrants—Civil rights—Italy. | Emigration and immigration law—Italy. | Emigration and immigration law—Libya. | Border security—European Union countries. |
Border security—Italy. | Italy—Foreign relations—Libya. |
Libya—Foreign relations—Italy.
Classification: LCC KJE6050 (ebook) | LCC KJE6050 .L54 2019 (print) | DDC 342.2408/2—dc23
LC record available at https://lccn.loc.gov/2018060411

ISBN 13: 978-1-03-224136-4 (pbk)
ISBN 13: 978-1-138-34348-1 (hbk)

DOI: 10.4324/9780429439100

Typeset in Times New Roman
by codeMantra

Contents

Preface

This work takes into account the law as it stood, to the best of the author's knowledge, on 5 December 2018. Part of the arguments discussed in the present work have been previously published in the *Rivista di Diritto Internazionale*, n. 4/2018, as a paper titled "The Externalization of Border Controls and the Responsibility of Outsourcing States under the European Convention on Human Rights". Moreover, I had the opportunity to discuss these issues during the Final International Conference of the 2017 Summer School of the Jean Monnet Centre of Excellence on Migrants' Rights in the Mediterranean (Chair: Professor Giuseppe Cataldi, University of Naples 'L'Orientale') held on 21 June 2017 in Castellammare di Stabia, Naples (talk titled "The 2017 Italy-Libya Memorandum and its consequences"), and in the course of the 2017 Annual Conference of The Society of Legal Scholars on "The Diverse Unity of Law", in the Section *Migration &Asylum Law* (Co-convenors: dr. Diego Acosta Arcarazo, University of Bristol and dr. Violeta Moreno-Lax, Queen Mary University of London), held in Dublin on 5 September 2017 (lecture titled "The externalization of border controls and the responsibility of outsourcing States").

I wish to thank all my colleagues, doctoral candidates and students for providing inspiration and motivation. In particular, I am very grateful to Prof. Giuseppe Cataldi for his constructive feedback and continuous support. Finally, a special thanks to my loved ones, Roberto and Marco.

Abbreviations

ASR	International Law Commission
	Draft Articles on the Responsibility of States
ECHR	European Convention on Human Rights
ECtHR	European Court of Human Rights
EU	European Union
CFSP	Common Foreign and Security Policy
CJEU	Court of Justice of the European Union
EUNAVFOR MED	European Union Naval Force Mediterranean
ICJ	International Court of Justice
ILC	International Law Commission
IMRCC	Italian Maritime Rescue Coordination Centre
IOM	International Organization for Migration
SAR	Search and Rescue zone
TEU	Treaty on the European Union
TFEU	Treaty on the Functioning of the European Union
UNHCR	United Nations High Commissioner for Refugees

Introduction

In order to deal with the growing number of migrants at their borders, many States have inaugurated or strengthened already existing practices of repression and deterrence to "stem" arrivals. These practices consist of criminalization and detention of irregular migrants, separation of family members, poor reception conditions, excessive prolongation of status determination, reduction of procedural safeguards, including not only expedited returns, but also fences, walls and, more and more, externalization of border controls.[1]

At this time, the externalization of migration border controls is no longer a novelty but rather a widespread practice, both at European and non-European levels.[2]

With specific regard to Europe, over the past few decades, both the European Union and European States have implemented various strategies to externalize border controls, such as visa requirements, carrier sanctions, high seas interceptions and 'safe third country' procedures, with the declared intent of saving human lives and countering trafficking, but with the actual end result of shifting borders, circumventing international obligations and ultimately preventing access to Europe.

1 See Report of the Special Rapporteur on torture and other cruel, inhuman or degrading treatment or punishment of 26 February 2018, Doc. A/HRC/37/50, available at https://www.ohchr.org/Documents/Issues/Torture/A_HRC_37_50_EN.pdf (accessed on 30 November 2018).

2 See, *ex multis*, Gammeltoft-Hansen, Thomas, Vedsted-Hansen, Jens (eds), *Human Rights and the Dark Side of Globalisation*, London and New York, Routledge, 2017 and, with specific regard to Europe: Gammeltoft-Hansen, Thomas, *Access to Asylum: International Refugee Law and the Globalisation of Migration Control*, Cambridge, Cambridge University Press, 2011; Den Heijer, Maarten, *Europe and Extraterritorial Asylum*, Oxford, Hart Publishing, 2012; Moreno-Lax, Violeta, *Accessing Asylum Europe: Extraterritorial Border Controls and Refugee Rights Under EU Law*, Oxford, Oxford University Press, 2017.

One of the main concerns regarding these policies is that they risk creating "legal black holes",[3] particularly worrisome since, as we have learned from Australian[4] and US[5] border control practices, externalization can lead to infringements of migrants' rights, in particular the prohibition of torture and inhuman treatment, the principle of *non-refoulement*, the right to leave any country, the right to liberty (arbitrary and prolonged detention), the right to seek asylum, the rights of vulnerable people (children, victims of trafficking etc.), and the right to effective remedies.[6] These risks are particularly likely due to the most recent evolution of this practice in Europe, because of the proliferation of arrangements with unsafe third countries – countries of origin or transit – delegated "to effect migration control on behalf of the developed world".[7] These arrangements appear to have been created with the explicit purpose of avoiding accountability, in particular to exclude jurisdiction under the European Convention on Human

---

3 Wilde, Ralph, "Legal "Black Hole"?: Extraterritorial State Action and International Treaty Law on Civil and Political Rights" in *Michigan Journal of International Law*, Vol. 26, N. 3, 2005, p. 739 ff.

4 See, *ex multis*, Kneebone, Susan, "The Pacific Plan: The Provision of 'Effective Protection'", in *International Journal of Refugee Law*, Vol.18, N. 3–4, 2006, p. 696 ff. and more recently, Hirsch, Asher, "The Borders Beyond the Border: Australia's Extraterritorial Migration Controls", in *Refugee Survey Quarterly*, Vol. 36, N. 3, 2017, p. 36 ff. On the influence of the Australian practice on Europe, see, in particular, McAdam, Jane, "Migrating Laws? The 'Plagiaristic Dialogue' between Europe and Australia", in *The Global Reach of European Refugee Law* (H. Lambert, J. McAdam, M. Fullerton eds), Cambridge, Cambridge University Press, 2013, p. 25 ff.

5 US management of migration flows has varied between *refoulement* (endorsed by the Supreme Court in the *Sale* judgment) and prescreening in the Naval Base of Guantanamo, in Jamaica, and Turks and Caicos, violating human rights for conditions of detention and giving rise to difficulties in accessing fair procedures and the risk of *refoulement* to unsafe countries. See, *ex multis*, Koh, Harold, "The 'Haiti Paradigm' in United States Human Rights Policy", in *Yale Law Journal*, Vol. 103, N. 8, 1994, p. 2391 ff.; Legomsky, Stephen H., "The USA and the Caribbean Interdiction Program", in *International Journal of Refugee Law*, Vol. 18, N. 3–4, 2006, p. 680 ff. On the *Sale* judgment, see, in particular, Goodwin-Gill, Guy S., "YLS Sale Symposium: The Globalization of High Seas Interdiction. Sale's Legacy and Beyond", in *OpinioJuris*, 16 March 2014, available at http://opiniojuris.org/2014/03/16/yale-sale-symposium-globalization-high-seas-interdiction-sales-legacy-beyond (accessed on 7 October 2018).

6 Frelick, Bill, Kysel, Ian M., Podkul, Jennifer, "The Impact of Externalization of Migration Controls on the Rights of Asylum Seekers and Other Migrants", in *Journal on Migration and Human Security*, Vol. 4, N. 4, 2016, p. 190 ff.

7 Gammeltoft-Hansen, Thomas, Hathaway, James C., "Non-Refoulement in a World of Cooperative Deterrence", in *Columbia Journal of Transnational Law*, 2015, p. 243.

Rights (ECHR),[8] especially in light of the well-known *Hirsi* judgment, a cornerstone for the respect of human rights for migrants and asylum seekers. In fact, the judgment of 23 February 2012,[9] handed down by the Grand Chamber of the European Court of Human Rights (ECtHR), stigmatized such externalization practices as interceptions on the high seas when conducted under the effective control of Contracting States.

It is the purpose of this work to verify whether European States can shift their responsibility onto Third States in cases of human rights violations with regard to the new and varied forms of "cooperation-based"[10] *non-entrée* policies, from the provision of financial, technical, technological support to third countries for the prevention of departures, to typologies of cooperation entailing a stronger and more direct involvement by European States, such as deployment of officials to countries of origin, or transit up to the assumption of a coordination role or even of a direct migration control role.

The present work will focus on a case study, the Italy-Libya Memorandum of Understanding of February 2017, which implements a new model of externalization, based on 'pull-backs' i.e. an evolution of the 'push-backs' practice repeatedly condemned by the ECtHR since the judgment handed down in the above mentioned *Hirsi* case. [11]

---

8 See De Vittor, Francesca, "Responsabilità degli Stati e dell'Unione europea nella conclusione e nell'esecuzione di 'accordi' per il controllo extraterritoriale della migrazione", in *Diritti umani e diritto internazionale*, 2018, p. 27.

9 ECtHR, *Hirsi Jamaa and Others v. Italy*, judgment of 23 February 2012 [GC], applic. No. 27765/09. On the *Hirsi* judgment, see Den Heijer, Maarten, "Reflections on Refoulement and Collective Expulsion in the Hirsi Case", in *International Journal of Refugee Law*, Vol. 25, N. 2, 2013, p. 265 ff.; Giuffré, Mariagiulia, "Watered-Down Rights on the High Seas: Hirsi Jamaa and Others v Italy", in *International & Comparative Law Quarterly*, Vol. 61, N. 3, 2012, p. 728 ff.; Liguori, Anna, "La Corte europea dei diritti dell'uomo condanna l'Italia per i respingimenti verso la Libia del 2009: il caso Hirsi", in *Rivista di Diritto internazionale*, Vol. 95, N. 2, 2012, p. 415 ff.; Messineo, Francesco, "Yet Another Mala Figura: Italy Breached Non-Refoulement Obligations by Intercepting Migrants' Boats at Sea, Says ECtHR", in *European Journal of Int. Law Talk!*, 24 February 2012, available at https://www.ejiltalk.org/yet-another-mala-figura-italy-breached-non-refoulement-obligations-by-intercepting-migrants-boats-at-sea-says-ecthr/ (accessed on 7 October 2018); Moreno-Lax, Violeta, "Hirsi v. Italy or the Strasbourg Court versus Extraterritorial Migration Control?", in *Human Rights Law Review*, Vol. 12, N. 3, 2012, p. 574 ff.; Napoletano, Nicola, "La condanna dei 'respingimenti' operati dall'Italia verso la Libia da parte della Corte europea dei diritti umani: molte luci e qualche ombra", in *Diritti umani e diritto internazionale*, Vol. 6, N. 2, 2012, p. 436 ff.

10 Gammeltoft-Hansen, Hathaway, cit., p. 243.

11 Most recently, in the judgment *N.D. and N.T. v. Spain* of 3 October 2017 (applic. Nos. 8675/15 and 8697/15): see Pijnenburg, Annick, "Is N.D. and N.T. v. Spain the new

As stated by the Special Rapporteur on torture and other cruel, inhuman or degrading treatment or punishment, Nils Melzer, in his Report of 26 February 2018[12]:

> Pullback operations are designed to physically prevent migrants from leaving the territory of their State of origin or a transit State (retaining State), or to forcibly return them to that territory, before they can reach the jurisdiction of their destination State [...]
>
> Most notably, while both retaining States and supportive destination States often portray 'pullbacks' as humanitarian operations aiming to 'rescue' migrants in distress from overcrowded and unseaworthy vessels at sea, or to prevent them from embarking on such 'unsafe journeys', or to 'defeat the business model of smugglers and traffickers', the well-documented reality is that intercepted migrants are generally returned to their port of departure, where they are routinely detained or further deported to unsafe third States and, in both cases, exposed to a substantial risk of torture and ill-treatment, or even death, without access to an assessment of their protection needs or any other legal remedy.

The 2017 MoU is emblematic of the risk of torture described by Special Rapporteur Melzer, because of the dire situation that migrants and asylum seekers face in Libya, as extensively documented by several UN and NGO Reports that will be explored in detail in the following paragraphs.

The primary responsibility of these serious violations is certainly upon Libya itself, and it is noteworthy that the Prosecutor of the International Criminal Court has clarified on a number of occasions that the ongoing investigations relating to Libya (following a referral by the UN Security Council) also concern "serious and widespread crimes against migrants attempting to transit through Libya".[13] The present

---

Hirsi?", in *European Journal of International Law: Talk!*, 17 October 2017, available at https://www.ejiltalk.org/is-n-d-and-n-t-v-spain-the-new-hirsi/ (accessed on 7 October 2018); Cellamare, Giovanni, "Note in margine alla sentenza della Corte europea dei diritti dell'uomo nell'affare N.D. e N.T. c. Spagna ", in *Studi sull'integrazione europea*, Vol. XIII, N. 1, 2018, p. 153 ff.; Salvadego, Laura, "I respingimenti sommari di migranti alle frontiere terrestri dell'enclave di Melilla", in *Diritti umani e diritto internazionale*, 2018, p. 199 ff.

12 Cit., para. 56.

13 See *Statement to the United Nations Security Council on the Situation in Libya, pursuant to UNSCR 1970 (2011)*, of 2 November 2018, para 15–16; of 8 May 2018, para 25–26; of 8 November 2017, para 31; of 9 May 2017, para 44, available at www.icc-cpi.int (accessed on 30 November 2018).

work will explore whether Italy is also responsible – focusing in particular on violation of the prohibition of torture – and what the basis of such responsibility under international law might be. To this end, I will primarily investigate the hypothesis of Italy's responsibility for complicity. In particular, I will verify whether the requirements laid out in Art. 16 of the *ILC Articles on the Responsibility of States* are met. Secondly, I will explore the benefit of applying the doctrine of positive obligations, as developed in the case law of the ECtHR, which could prove to be a particularly useful tool in addressing the responsibility of European States under the ECHR within an externalized context, in that it may make it easier to meet the jurisdiction requirement and ultimately hold outsourcing States accountable.

The second part of the work will examine the Italy-Libya MoU within the broader scenario of EU policies on extraterritorial border controls.

A quick overview of the recent decisions of the European Court of Justice vis-à-vis two aspects of EU externalization – i.e the two EU-Turkey orders (the General Court order of 28 February 2017 and the European Court of Justice order of 12 September 2018 on appeal) and the Humanitarian Visa Judgment of 7 March 2017 – will pave the way for the conclusions since, as I will try to demonstrate, the current attitude of the Luxembourg Court confirms the importance of focusing on the responsibility of European States, with particular regard to the possibility of bringing claims against Italy – and against outsourcing States in general – before the ECtHR.

Part I

A case study

The 2017 Italy-Libya
Memorandum of Understanding

1   The Italy-Libya Memorandum of 2 February 2017

On 2 February 2017, Italy signed a highly controversial *Memorandum of Understanding on Cooperation in the Field of Development, Fight against Illegal Immigration, Trafficking in Human Beings and Smuggling and on Enhancement of Border Security*[1] with Fayez Mustafa Serraj, President of the Council of the Libyan Government of National Accord.[2] The intensification of crossings through the Central Mediterranean Route to Italy in 2016, due to the closure of the Balkan route and the implementation of the EU-Turkey deal,[3] is the reason for the new policy approach aimed at stopping sea arrivals at any cost, in a misguided attempt to deal with the growing hostility of Italian public opinion vis-à-vis migrants. Italy's initiative was very welcomed by the European Union, which, in the Malta Declaration of 3 February 2017, expressed its explicit endorsement of the MoU and its readiness to support Italy in its implementation.[4]

As pointed out, "the key commitments of the partnership… is to resume the cooperation between Italy and Libya on security and

---

1 Italian text available at http://www.governo.it/sites/governo.it/files/Libia.pdf; unofficial translation in English at http://eumigrationlawblog.eu/wp-content/uploads/2017/10/MEMORANDUM_translation_finalversion.doc.pdf (accessed on 30 November 2018).

2 The Libyan Government of National Accord, born in January 2016, has been recognized as "the sole legitimate government of Libya" not only by the UN (whose mediation was essential for the establishment of the said Libyan Government), but also by the African Union, the EU and many states, including Italy. Since 2014, however, Libya has been divided into competing political and military factions and during the second half of 2018, instability became increasingly worse.

3 See part II, § 1.2.

4 See Malta Declaration, para. 6 lett. i), available at https://www.consilium.europa.eu/en/press/press-releases/2017/02/03/malta-declaration/ (accessed on 7 October 2018). The EU scenario will be further explored in the second part of this work.

irregular migration according to past bilateral agreements",[5] i.e. the *Treaty of Friendship, Partnership and Cooperation* signed in 2008 between Italy and Libya,[6] which had opened the door to the push-backs of boat-refugees to Libya in 2009. This resulted in the well-known 2012 *Hirsi* judgment of the ECtHR,[7] concerning the interception at sea and push-backs to Libya of eleven Somalians and thirteen Eritreans by the Italian Revenue Police (Guardia di Finanza) and the Coastguard. With this judgment, the ECtHR condemned Italy for violation of Article 3 ECHR (prohibition of torture and inhuman and degrading treatment), Art. 4 of Protocol No. 4 (prohibition of collective expulsions), and Article 13 (right to an effective remedy) taken in conjunction with Arts. 3 and 4 of Protocol No. 4. The 2008 Treaty had been suspended in 2011 after the fall of the Gaddafi regime and the subsequent civil war.

The 2017 MoU is composed of 8 articles and a preamble. Articles 1 and 2 outline the obligations of the parties; Article 3 envisages the institution of a mixed committee to implement the MoU; Article 4 concerns the financing; Article 5 contains a referral to international obligations and human rights; and Articles 6 to 8 regard the amendment procedure, the settlement of disputes and the duration of the agreement (three years).

First of all, it must be said that the memorandum adopts an unacceptable language, both from a formal and a substantial point of view. Indeed, it refers always to "illegal" or "clandestine" migrants, although the General Assembly of the United Nations has recommended the use of the terms "undocumented" or "irregular" migrants since 1975.[8] But what is more disquieting is the fact that it does not make any reference to refugees and asylum seekers, even though it is well known that migration flows from Libya are mixed.

5 See Palm, Anja, "The Italy-Libya Memorandum of Understanding: The Baseline of a Policy Approach Aimed at Closing All Doors to Europe?", in *EU Immigration and Asylum Law and Policy*, 2 October 2017, available at http://eumigrationlawblog.eu/the-italy-libya-memorandum-of-understanding-the-baseline-of-a-policy-approach-aimed-at-closing-all-doors-to-europe/ (accessed on 7 October 2018).
6 Ronzitti, Natalino, "Italia-Libia: il Trattato di Bengasi e la sua effettiva rilevanza", in *Affari Internazionali Blog*, 14 July 2018, available at http://www.affarinternazionali.it/2018/07/italia-libia-trattato-bengasi/ (accessed on 7 October 2018).
7 See supra p. 4, note 9.
8 Since Resolution 3449(XXX) *Measures to improve the situation and ensure the human rights and dignity of all migrant workers*, available at http://repository.un.org/handle/11176/151614 (accessed on 7 October 2018).

Moreover, it is quite vague with regard to the amount and origin of funding,[9] simply stating that Italy will provide for the financing of the initiatives, in addition to making use of available funds from the European Union, "without additional obligations for the Italian State's budget". This provision was probably introduced to avoid allegations of violation of Article 80 of the Italian Constitution, which provides that treaties entailing expenses not included in the national budget cannot be concluded in simplified form but require the authorization of Parliament. However, as noted,[10] since Article 80 of the Italian Constitution also states that "treaties of political nature" must be concluded in solemn form, and given that the MoU involves fundamental foreign policy choices of great political relevance, an allegation of violation of Article 80 of the Italian Constitution is not precluded by the formulation of Article 8.[11] Indeed, in February 2018, a claim was lodged before the Constitutional Court by four Italian deputies. In July 2018, the Constitutional Court declared the recourse inadmissible without examining it on merits[12] as it concerns "prerogatives which – by specific Constitutional requirement – is the responsibility of the Assembly as a whole, not its individual component. Only the Assembly may assess whether to take action regarding possible violations".[13]

The core of the deal is represented by Articles 1 and 2, which state in very clear terms that the Parties agree to start cooperation initiatives with the explicit aim of *stemming the illegal migrants' fluxes*[14] and that to this end, Italy will provide, *inter alia*, "technical and technological support to the Libyan institutions in charge of the fight against illegal immigration … ", finance "reception centres already active" and train Libyan personnel.

---

9 See Palm, cit.

10 Mancini, Marina, "Italy's New Migration Control Policy: Stemming the Flow of Migrants from Libya Without Regard for Their Human Rights", in *Italian Yearbook of International Law*, Vol. XXVII, 2018, p. 262.

11 On compliance with internal rules concerning the procedure for the conclusion of treaties, see also De Vittor, "Responsabilità degli Stati", cit., p. 9–10.

12 See order n. 163/2018, available at https://www.cortecostituzionale.it/actionScheda Pronuncia.do;jsessionid=86937CC338DC604BFB8B5541980E1432 (accessed on 30 November 2018). On this order, see Lauro, Alessandro, "Il conflitto fra poteri dello Stato e la forma di governo parlamentare: a margine delle ordinanze 163 e 181 del 2018", in *Quaderni Costituzionali*, 2018, available at http://www.forumcostituzionale. it/wordpress/wp-content/uploads/2018/10/nota_163_181_2018_lauro.pdf (accessed on 7 October 2018).

13 Unofficial translation from Italian.

14 Article 1. Italics added.

As will be analyzed in the next paragraph, the most critical aspect of the MoU is the complete indifference to human rights, notwithstanding the rhetorical reference to human rights provided for in Article 5 of the MoU. Libya is not a signatory of the 1951 refugee Convention, a domestic regime for people in need of international protection is completely lacking and, above all, widespread violations and abuses vis-à-vis migrants in Libya had already been attested to by the European Court of Human Rights (ECtHR) in the abovementioned *Hirsi* judgement. With this decision, the Strasbourg Court found Italy responsible for violation of Article 3 of the European Convention on Human Rights (ECHR) for having taken intercepted migrants back to Libya specifically because of the inhuman treatment to which those people were subjected once they returned, with regard both to the conditions in the Libyan detention centres and to the risk of being sent back to the countries from which they were fleeing (indirect *refoulement*). Since that time, the risk of abuse of migrants in Libya has become increasingly worse, as will be examined in the next paragraph. Nevertheless, not only is any positive conditionality missing from the 2017 MoU (i.e. there is no clause making the aid subject to the improvement of human rights conditions and to the ratification of the Geneva Convention), but the cooperation aims explicitly at empowering Libyan authorities to pull migrants back to the hell in Libya. The only difference with the *Hirsi* case is that Italy will not be doing so by itself, aware that this might be contrary to the ECHR, but will be providing technical, technological and financial aid to Libya, in effect attaining the same result. In other words, Italy is doing "refoulement by proxy",[15] to circumvent the prohibition unequivocally affirmed by the ECtHR in the abovementioned *Hirsi* judgment. An unambiguous confirmation of this is in the words of Italian Admiral Enrico Credendino, who in an interview for the Italian magazine, *Internazionale*,[16] stated:

> We will create a Libyan system capable of stopping migrants before they reach international waters, as a result *it will no longer be considered a push-back* because it will be the Libyans who will be rescuing the migrants and doing *whatever they consider appropriate with the migrants*[17].

15 See the report *Mare Clausum*, by Forensic Oceanography (Charles Heller and Lorenzo Pezzani), affiliated to the Forensic Architecture agency, Goldsmiths, University of London, May 2018.
16 The video is available at https://www.internazionale.it/video/2017/05/04/ong-libia-migranti (accessed on 30 November 2018). The quotation starts at 3'51".
17 Unofficial translation from Italian.

The aim of this work is precisely to demonstrate that European States – in this particular case, Italy – cannot shift their responsibility under international law to Third States, at least with respect to the rule of customary international law prohibiting torture and inhuman treatment, which, as anticipated, will be the focus of this work.[18] Of course, in the specific case under examination, the best way of respecting human rights should have been to give no support at all to Libya. In point of fact, during the months of July and August 2017, Libya started to implement the said agreement and arrivals of migrants to Italy's coast decreased significantly. Such a result, however, was reached at the expense of migrants' human rights, since, as examined in the next paragraph, people pulled back to Libya were (and still are) exposed to very serious violations of human rights.

---

18 On the possible violation of "the right to leave", see Markard, Nora, "The Right to Leave by Sea: Legal Limits on EU Migration Control by Third Countries", in *European Journal of Migration and Law*, Vol. 27, N. 3, 2016, p. 591 ff. and Moreno-Lax, Violeta, Giuffré, Mariagiulia, "The Rise of Consensual Containment: From 'Contactless Control' to 'Contactless Responsibility' for Forced Migration Flows", in *Research Handbook on International Refugee Law* (Juss ed), Cheltenham, forthcoming, available at https://papers.ssrn.com/sol3/papers.cfm?abstract_id=3009331 (accessed on 7 October 2018).

2 Violations of human rights in Libya

As anticipated above, the 2012 European Court of Human Rights (ECtHR) *Hirsi* judgment is an authoritative jurisprudential precedent indirectly attesting to serious human rights violations in Libya vis-à-vis migrants. Since then, however, the risk of abuse of migrants in Libya has become increasingly worse, due, *inter alia*, to the deterioration of the political situation after the fall of Gaddafi in 2011. With regard to the period immediately before the signing of the MoU, we refer to the report of 1 December 2016[1] of the Secretary-General on the United Nations Support Mission in Libya (UNSMIL),[2] which attests that:

> Migrants detained in centres operated by the [Libyan] Department did not go through any legal process, and there was no oversight by judicial authorities. Conditions in the centres were inhuman, with people held in warehouses in appalling sanitary conditions, with poor ventilation and extremely limited access to light and water. In some detention centres, migrants suffered from severe malnutrition, and UNSMIL received numerous and consistent reports of torture, including beatings and sexual violence, as well as forced labour by armed groups with access to the centres.

Several other reports went in the same direction. The report of the UNSMIL and the Office of the United Nations High Commissioner for Human Rights (OHCHR), released on 13 December 2016, significantly titled "Detained and dehumanised. Report on human rights abuses

---

1 United Nations Security Council, *Report of the Secretary-General on the United Nations Support Mission in Libya*, 1 December 2016, Doc. S/2016/1011, para. 41, available at http://undocs.org/S/2016/1011 (accessed on 7 October 2018).
2 Pursuant to Security Council resolution 2291 (2016), which decided to extend the mandate of UNSMIL (including inter alia human rights monitoring and reporting).

against migrants in Libya", which states that "OHCHR considers migrants to be at high risk of suffering serious human rights violations, including arbitrary detention, in Libya and thus *urges States not to return, or facilitate the return of, persons to Libya*"[3]; the European Border Assistance Mission (EUBAM) Libya Initial Mapping Report of January 2017,[4] which mentions gross human rights violations and extreme abuse (including sexual abuse, slavery, torture) vis-à-vis migrants detained in Libyan camps; the Human Rights Watch World Report 2017, published on 12 January 2017, revealing that in Libya, "Officials and militias held migrants and refugees in prolonged detention without judicial review and subjected them to poor conditions, including overcrowding and insufficient food. Guards and militia members subjected migrants and refugees to beatings, forced labour, and sexual violence".[5] Also noteworthy is the United Nations High Commissioner for Refugees-International Organization for Migration (UNHCR-IOM) joint statement[6] addressing migration and refugee movements along the Central Mediterranean route, delivered on 2 February 2017, in which both organizations declared "We believe that, given the current context, it is not appropriate to consider Libya a safe third country nor to establish extraterritorial processing of asylum-seekers in North Africa".

The situation did not improve in the following months, as asserted by numerous reports published after the signing of the MoU: the Final Report of the Panel of Experts on Libya – established pursuant to the UN Security Council resolution 1973 (2011) – , transmitted to the UN Security Council on 1 June 2017[7]; the report published on 15 August 2017, by UN Special Rapporteur on extrajudicial, summary or arbitrary executions, Agnes Callamard, on the "Unlawful Death of Refugees and Migrants"[8]; the UN Secretary-General's Report of 22

---

3 http://www.ohchr.org/Documents/Countries/LY/DetainedAndDehumanised_en.pdf, p. 12. Italics added (accessed on 7 October 2018).
4 http://www.statewatch.org/news/2017/jun/eu-eeas-strategic-review-libya-9202-17.pdf (accessed on 7 October 2018).
5 https://www.hrw.org/world-report/2017/country-chapters/libya (accessed on 7 October 2018).
6 http://www.unhcr.org/news/press/2017/2/58931ffb4/joint-unhcr-iomstatement-addressing-migration-refugee-movements-along.html (accessed on 7 October 2018).
7 Which highlights, *inter alia*, links between armed groups, criminal groups and different coast guard factions (in some cases, even the involvement of the Libyan coastguard in human smuggling activities) and ill treatment and forced labour of intercepted migrants: http://undocs.org/S/2017/466 (accessed on 7 October 2018).
8 http://www.un.org/en/ga/search/view_doc.asp?symbol=A/72/335 (accessed on 7 October 2018).

August 2017 on the UNSMIL[9]; the Report of the Secretary-General pursuant to Security Council resolution 2312 (2016), of 7 September 2017[10]; the Statement of 14 November 2017 by UN High Commissioner for Human Rights, Zeid Ra'ad Al Hussein.[11]

Particularly interesting is the above-mentioned UN Secretary-General's Report of 22 August 2017, which states that "Migrants continued to be subjected by smugglers, traffickers, members of armed groups and security forces to extreme violence; torture and other ill-treatment; forced labour; arbitrary deprivation of liberty; rape; and other sexual violence and exploitation"; that IOM had denounced the presence of slave markets in Libya concerning sub-Saharans migrants; that the International Criminal Court informed the Security Council that it was carefully examining the feasibility of opening an investigation into migrant-related crimes in Libya. What is additionally important to stress is that the document apprises of "dangerous, life-threatening interceptions by armed men believed to be from the Libyan Coast Guard", as those actions are the direct consequence of the above-mentioned MoU. The report adds that "UNSMIL has been reviewing its support to the Libyan Coast Guard in line with the United Nations human rights due diligence policy", which renders even more striking the indifference conversely shown by Italy (and by the European Union in general, as will be examined in the second part of the book), to the blatant and well-documented human rights violations of migrants pulled back to Libya.

In 2018, the situation has not significantly changed, as attested *inter alia* by the report *Abuse Behind Bars: Arbitrary and unlawful detention in Libya*,[12] published in April 2018 by the OHCHR in cooperation with the UNSMIL; the *UNHCR Position on Returns to Libya - Update II*[13] of September 2018; the UNHCR Statement of 23 November 2018, which reiterates that "[i]n light of the dangers for refugees and migrants in

---

9 https://unsmil.unmissions.org/sites/default/files/n1725784.pdf, in particular para. 34–36 (accessed on 7 October 2018).

10 http://undocs.org/S/2017/761(accessed on 7 October 2018).

11 https://www.ohchr.org/en/NewsEvents/Pages/DisplayNews.aspx?NewsID=22393 (accessed on 7 October 2018). Also the Council of Europe Commissioner for Human Rights, Nils Muižnieks, expressed his concern about the Italian cooperation with Libya: see the letter sent by Nils Muižnieks to the Minister of the Interior of Italy (and the reply of the Minister of the Interior of Italy) at https://www.coe.int/en/web/commissioner/-/commissioner-seeks-clarifications-over-italy-s-maritime-operations-in-libyan-territorial-waters?desktop=true (accessed on 7 October 2018).

12 https://www.ohchr.org/Documents/Countries/LY/AbuseBehindBarsArbitrary-Unlawful_EN.pdf (accessed on 7 October 2018).

13 http://www.refworld.org/docid/5b8d02314.html (accessed on 7 October 2018).

Libya, UNHCR does not consider it to be a safe place for disembarkation and also has advised against returns to Libya following search
and rescues at sea".[14]

Among the numerous NGO Reports, it is important to single out
the Amnesty International report "Libya's dark web of collusion",[15]
published in December 2017, and its Public Statement of November
2018, asserting that "the situation for migrants and refugees in the
country remains bleak and, in some respects, has worsened".[16]

14 https://www.unhcr.org/news/press/2018/11/5bf7e0634/unhcr-appeals-resettlement-
end-detention-libya-evacuations-near-2500.html (accessed on 7 October 2018).
15 https://www.amnesty.org/download/Documents/MDE1975612017ENGLISH.PDF
(accessed on 7 October 2018).
16 https://www.amnesty.org/en/latest/news/2018/11/cruel-european-migration-policies-
leave-refugees-trapped-in-libya-with-no-way-out/ (accessed on 7 October 2018).

3 Italy's responsibility for complicity

Since the signing of the above-mentioned MoU, scholars have been investigating Italy's responsibility on the basis of complicity.[1] This chapter will therefore first analyze the notion of complicity under

1 Gauci, Jean-Pierre, "Back to Old Tricks? Italian Responsibility for Returning People to Libya", in *European Journal of International Law Talk!*, 6 June 2017, available at https://www.ejiltalk.org/back-to-old-tricks-italian-responsibility-for-returning-people-to-libya/ (accessed on 7 October 2018); Carella, Gabriella, "Il sonno della ragione genera politiche migratorie", in *SIDIBlog*, 11 September 2017, available at http://www.docentilex.uniba.it/docenti-1/gabriella-carella/corsi/diritto-internazionale-Img-a-l/parte-speciale/CARELLA%20SIDIblog.pdf (accessed on 7 October 2018); Moreno-Lax, Giuffré, cit.; De Vittor, "Responsabilità degli Stati", cit.; Pascale, Giuseppe, "«Esternalizzazione» delle frontiere in chiave antimigratoria e responsabilità internazionale dell'Italia e dell'UE per complicità nelle gross violations dei diritti umani commesse in Libia", in *Studi sull'integrazione europea*, Vol. XIII, 2018, p. 413 ff.; Palladino, Rossana, "Nuovo quadro di partenariato dell'Unione europea per la migrazione e profili di responsabilità dell'Italia (e dell'Unione europea) in riferimento al caso libico", in *Freedom, Security & Justice: European Legal Studies*, 2018, p. 104 ff., available at http://www.fsjeurostudies.eu/files/FSJ.2018.II.Palladino_DEF5.pdf (accessed on 7 October 2018); Mackenzie-Gray Scott, Richard, "Torture in Libya and Questions of EU Member State Complicity", in *European Journal of International Law: Talk!*, 11 January 2018, available at https://www.ejiltalk.org/torture-in-libya-and-questions-of-eu-member-state-complicity/ (last accessed on 7 October 2018); Mancini, cit; Skordas, Achilles, "A 'Blind Spot' in the Migration Debate? International Responsibility of the EU and Its Member States for Cooperating with the Libyan Coastguard and Militias", in *EU Immigration and Asylum Law and Policy*, 30 January 2018, available at http://eumigrationlawblog.eu/a-blind-spot-in-the-migration-debate-international-responsibility-of-the-eu-and-its-member-states-for-cooperating-with-the-libyan-coastguard-and-militias/ (last accessed on 7 October 2018); Dastyari, Azadeh, Hirsch, Asher (n.d.). "The Ring of Steel: Extraterritorial Migration Controls in Indonesia and Libya and the Complicity of Australia and Italy", in *Human Rights Law Review* (forthcoming), available at https://www.academia.edu/37586230/The_Ring_of_Steel_Extraterritorial_Migration_Controls_in_Indonesia_and_Libya_and_the_Complicity_of_Australia_and_Italy (accessed on 27 November 2018).

international law and then explore whether Italy should be held indirectly responsible for complicity.

The provision of a rule on complicity is an important step for the rule of law. As pointed out,[2] the notion of complicity "heralds the extension of legal responsibility into areas where States have previously carried moral responsibility but the law has not clearly rendered them responsible for the acts that they facilitate". However, since not all forms of cooperation fulfil the requirements for complicity, I will first examine the notion of complicity as established in Article 16 of the International Law Commission Draft Articles on the Responsibility of States (hereafter, ASR).[3] Indeed, the actual Article 16 provided for in the ASR is entitled *Aid or assistance in the commission of an internationally wrongful act*; conversely, the initial proposal of Rapporteur Ago in 1978[4] used the term 'complicity', but in the following draft of Article 27[5] the term transmuted into 'aid and assistance', as this was deemed more neutral.[6]

Although the First report of Rapporteur Ago clearly affirmed that the provision would be only part of the progressive development of international law,[7] in the *Bosnian Genocide* case, the International Court of Justice (hereafter, ICJ) held that responsibility for aid or assistance under Article 16 ASR is a rule of customary international law.[8] However, the ICJ did not quote any State practice to support this

---

2 Lowe, Vaughan, *International Law*, Oxford, Oxford University Press, 2007, p. 121.

3 ILC Articles on the Responsibility of States for Internationally Wrongful Acts [2001] (hereafter ASR), YILC Vol. II (Part 2), Annex to UNGA Res. 56/83, 12 Dec. 2001 (A/56/49(Vol. I)/Corr.4).

4 Article 25: Complicity of a State in the internationally wrongful act of another State: see Ago, Roberto, 'Seventh Report on State Responsibility', ILC *Yearbook* 1978/II(1), p. 60.

5 Article 27: Aid or assistance by a State to another State for the commission of an internationally wrongful act: see ILC *Yearbook* 1987/II(2), p. 102.

6 Lanovoy, Vladyslav, "Complicity in an International Wrongful Act", SHARES Research Paper 38, 2014, p. 4, available at http://www.sharesproject.nl/wp-content/uploads/2014/03/SHARES-RP-38-final.pdf (accessed on 7 October 2018).

7 See Ago, cit. See also Crawford, James, *State Responsibility: The General Part*, Cambridge, Cambridge University Press, 2013, p. 13.

8 *Application of the Convention on the Prevention and Punishment of the Crime of Genocide (Bosnia and Herzegovina v. Serbia and Montenegro)*, Judgment, ICJ Reports 2007, p. 43 (hereafter, *Bosnian Genocide*) at para. 420. Previously, judge Stephen M. Schwebel had already come to the same conclusion in his dissenting opinion in the Nicaragua case (see ICJ, Military and Paramilitary Activities In and Against Nicaragua, Jurisdiction, Dissenting Opinion of Stephen W. Schwebel, ICJ Rep. 1984, p. 558, at para. 74). In the same direction, the vast majority of scholars: see Quigley, John, "Complicity in International Law: A New Direction in the Law of State Responsibility", in *The British Yearbook of International Law*, Vol. 57, N. 1,

position and it is not possible from the judgment "to infer the exact content of the rule".[9] As pointed out,[10] we can conclude from practice and *opinio juris* "that the current regime on responsibility for complicity contains more questions than answers".[11] The present chapter will thus attempt to explore some of the more problematic aspects.

3.1 Article 16 of the International Law Commission Draft Articles on the Responsibility of States (ASR)

Article 16 ASR states:

> Aid or assistance in the commission of an internationally wrongful act
>
> A State which aids or assists another State in the commission of an internationally wrongful act by the latter is internationally responsible for doing so if:
>
> (a) that State does so with knowledge of the circumstances of the internationally wrongful act; and
>
> (b) the act would be internationally wrongful if committed by that State.

In theory, 'aid and assistance' includes every act which facilitates the commission of an internationally wrongful act by another State.[12]

1986, p. 81–107; Graefrath, Bernhard, "Complicity in the Law of International Responsibility", in *Revue Belge de Droit International*, 1996/2, p. 378 ff.; Nahapetian, Kate, "Confronting State Complicity in International Law", in *UCLA Journal of International Law and Foreign Affairs*, Vol. 7, 2002, p. 101–104; Nolte, Georg, Aust, Helmut Philippe, "Equivocal Helpers: Complicit States, Mixed Messages and International Law", in *International and Comparative Law Quarterly*, Vol. 58, N. 1, 2009, p. 7-10; Aust, Helmut P., *Complicity and the Law of State Responsibility*, Cambridge, Cambridge University Press, 2011, p. 98; Lanovoy, cit., p. 2; Jackson, Miles, *Complicity in International Law*, Oxford, Oxford University Press, 2015, p. 150 ss.; De Wet, Erika, "Complicity in the Violations of Human Rights and Humanitarian Law by Incumbent Governments Through Direct Military Assistance on Request", in *International and Comparative Law Quarterly*, Vol. 67, N. 2, 2018, p. 290.

9 Aust, cit., p. 100.

10 Lanovoy, cit., p. 2.

11 Lanovoy, cit., p. 2.

12 More controversial still is the question of whether complicity can consist in omission, as per the statement of the ICJ in the Bosnian Genocide case: "while complicity results from commission, violation of the obligation to prevent results from omission" (p. 222, para. 432). On this point, see Lanovoy, cit., p. 11 and literature quoted therein.

Categories of acts which might fall within the scope of Article 16 are not only economic aid, the use of a state's territory or military bases, overflight, military procurement, the training of personnel and the provision of confidential information, but also the provision of aid of a legal or political nature, such as the conclusion of treaties which may facilitate the commission by the other party of a wrongful act.[13] The International Law Commission (hereafter, ILC) commentary explicitly alleges as example providing "material aid to a State that uses the aid to commit human rights violations".[14]

The ILC has not specifically defined what is considered as 'aid and assistance', but has clarified that "there is no requirement that the aid or assistance should have been essential to the performance of the internationally wrongful act; it is sufficient if it contributed significantly to the act".[15] As pointed out,[16] "no limitation is placed on the precise form of the aid or assistance in question – all that is required is a causative contribution to the illegal act". However, the degree and extent of contribution is important in distinguishing complicity from joint responsibility. On this point, the ILC Commentary states that in most cases of collaborative conduct by States, responsibility will be assessed according to the principle of independent responsibility and that only in exceptional cases can one State assume responsibility for the internationally wrongful act of another.[17] Indeed, "in theory, the distinction is one of attribution. Whereas in the scenario of joint or several responsibility the act causing the injury is concurrently attributable to two or more states, in the situation of complicity no attribution of the principal wrongful act to the complicit entity takes place".[18] In practice, however, the distinction between joint responsibility and complicity may be difficult, depending on the degree and extent of collaboration. For instance, it has been argued, with regard to complicity in aggression, that "The supply of weapons, military aircraft, radar equipment, and so forth, would in certain situations amount to 'aid or assistance'" while "the supply of combat units, vehicles equipment and personnel for the specific purpose of assisting an aggressor, would constitute a joint responsibility".[19]

13 ILC *Yearbook* 1987/II(2), p. 102.
14 ILC Commentary, Article 16, p. 67, para. 9.
15 ILC Commentary, Article 16, p. 66, para. 5.
16 Crawford, *State Responsibility*, cit., p. 402.
17 ILC Commentary, p. 64, para. 5.
18 Lanovoy, cit., p. 10.
19 Brownlie, Ian, *System of the Law of Nations: State Responsibility Part 1*, Oxford, Oxford University Press, 1983, p. 191.

The ILC Commentary further distinguishes complicity from the hypothesis of violation of an obligation to prevent certain conduct by another State and to this end quotes the *Corfu Channel* case,[20] where the ICJ held Albania responsible for its failure to warn the United Kingdom of the existence of mines (positioned by a third State, Yugoslavia), noting that in this case, "Albania's responsibility in the circumstances was original and not derived from the wrongfulness of the conduct of any other State".[21] However, as we will see, the categories of complicity and due diligence also are not always easy to distinguish and can overlap.[22]

3.1.1 The mental element

The most debated aspect of the concept of complicity as laid down in Article 16 ILC is the requirement that the act be committed "with knowledge of the circumstances of the internationally wrongful act". This uncertainty must, to a certain extent, be attributed to the ILC itself, as the requirement is set in three different ways. In point of fact, while Article 16 requires *"knowledge of the circumstances of the internationally wrongful act"*, the ILC's Commentary not only calls for the party assisting the State to be "aware of the circumstances making the conduct of the assisted State internationally wrongful", but also says that the aid must be given *"with a view to facilitating"* an internationally wrongful act (at paragraph 1), adding, at paragraph 5, that a State is not responsible unless the relevant organ *"intended ... to facilitate* the occurrence of the wrongful conduct".

The ongoing debate regards a number of issues: *inter alia* whether Article 16 ASR refers to knowledge of the unlawfulness of the assisted conduct or rather to knowledge of the factual circumstances making it unlawful; whether "actual or near certain knowledge" is mandatory or it is sufficient for there to be a constructive knowledge; the consequences of "wilful blindness"[23]; whether "intent" is an essential element of Article 16. With regard, in particular, to the last point,

---

20 *Corfu Channel (United Kingdom of Great Britain and Northern Ireland v. Albania)*, Judgment, ICJ Reports 1949, p. 4.
21 ILC Commentary, p. 64, para. 4.
22 See Aust, cit., p. 401. See *ultra* § 4.1.
23 The term, not present in either Article 16 ASR or in the ILC Commentary, "might be defined as a deliberate effort by the assisting State to avoid knowledge of illegality on the part of the State being assisted, in the face of credible evidence of present or future illegality": see Moynihan, Harriet, "Aiding and Assisting: The Mental Element under Article 16 of the International Law Commission's Articles on State Responsibility", in *International & Comparative Law Quarterly*, Vol. 67, N. 2, 2017, p. 461.

on the one hand, some scholars have argued that "the interpretation should be led by the goal not to discourage many typical forms of international cooperation which, on the whole, have more beneficial than adverse effects"[24] and have suggested that the mental element is to be interpreted as "wrongful intent". On the other hand, a number of arguments have been raised against such interpretation. As pointed out, "The obvious argument is that when a provision that is not in the Articles on State Responsibility appears in the ILC Commentary to the Articles, greater attention should be paid to the text of the articles, unless the discrepancy was discussed in plenary and the provision is nonetheless adopted in the Commentary (which was not the case with Article 16)".[25] In addition, some scholars[26] have argued that an intent requirement would make Article 16 unworkable – because it would be difficult to determine the frame of mind of a State – and that the assisting State seldom has a specific desire to aid the receiving State in committing a wrongful act, in particular, human rights violations: as pointed out, "[t]he problem is not so much one of 'intent' but of "deliberative indifference".[27]

So far, the mental requirement has yet to receive in-depth judicial consideration and the few phrases dedicated to it by the ICJ in the *Bosnian Genocide* case have been the object of contrasting interpretations. Indeed, at paragraph 421 of the above-mentioned judgment, the ICJ stated that 'at the least' complicity requires knowledge. Some scholars[28] have inferred from this that, in general, complicity requires more than knowledge, but as persuasively pointed out, this is not "the natural interpretation".[29] It might well be taken as simply implying that knowledge is usually sufficient. This leads us to a third position, that lessens the difference between 'knowledge' and 'intent', applying by analogy, the definition of intent provided for in the second part of sub-paragraph (b) of Article 30(2) of the Statute to the

---

24 See Nolte, Aust, cit., p. 15.
25 See Moynihan, cit., p. 465, quoting Gaja Giorgio, "Interpreting Articles Adopted by the International Law Commission", in *British Yearbook of International Law*, Vol. 85, N. 1, 2015, p. 10 ff. The latter explicitly refers to the discrepancy between Article 16 and the ILC Commentary, noting that in this case, the discrepancy was not discussed in plenary.
26 See Quigley, cit., p. 111.
27 See Gibney, Mark, Tomasevski, Katarina, Vedsted-Hansen, Jens, "Transnational State Responsibility for Violations of Human Rights", in *Harvard Human Rights Journal*, Vol. 12, 1999, p. 294.
28 See Aust, cit., p. 236; Crawford, *State Responsibility*, cit., p. 407.
29 Jackson, cit., p. 160.

International Criminal Court, which states that "A person has intent where:...(b) in relation to a consequence, that person means to cause that consequence or *is aware that it will occur in the ordinary course of events*".[30] As pointed out,[31] this provision illustrates a

> more oblique form of intent, where a person does not have the desire or will to bring about the consequences of the crime but is aware that those elements will be the almost inevitable outcome of his or her acts or omissions.

Finally, it is noteworthy to underline that Article 41 (2) of ILC rules, in contrast to Article 16, does not mention either knowledge or intent.

Indeed, Article 41 (2) states that:

2. No State shall recognize as lawful a situation created by a serious breach within the meaning of Article 40, nor render *aid or assistance* in maintaining that situation.

Thus, in case of serious violations of obligations "arising under a peremptory norm of general international law",[32] it was convincingly argued that "there is a stronger rule against complicity",[33] although it is not clear whether Article 41 (2) corresponds to general international law.[34]

This provision, as we will see, might also apply to the present case – because Libya has been accused of crimes against humanity vis-à-vis migrants[35] – and might therefore be invoked as an additional argument for affirming Italy's responsibility.

3.1.2 *The requirement of opposability*

Article 16 (b) sets out that a State which aids or assists another State in the commission of an internationally wrongful act by the latter is

---

30 Italics added.
31 Moynihan, cit., p. 467–468.
32 Article 40 ASR. For a thorough analysis of this provision, see Picone, Paolo, "Obblighi *erga omnes* e codificazione della responsabilità degli Stati", in *Rivista di diritto internazionale*, Vol. 88, N. 4, 2005, p. 893 ff.
33 Nolte, Aust, cit., p. 16. This is motivated by the ILC Commentary by the fact that "it is hardly conceivable that a State would not have notice of the commission of a serious breach by another State": see ILC Commentary, p. 115, para. 11
34 See Aust, cit., p. 343 and literature quoted therein at note n. 123.
35 See, most recently, the Sixteenth Report of the Prosecutor of the International Criminal Court to the United Nations Security Council pursuant to UNSCR 1970 (2011), para. 33, available at https://www.icc-cpi.int/itemsDocuments/181102-rep-otp-UNSC-libya_ENG.pdf (accessed on 30 November 2018).

internationally responsible for doing so if "the act would be internationally wrongful if committed by that State".

As stated in the Commentary, the rationale is that "a State cannot do by another what it cannot do by itself".[36] Therefore, the act must constitute a breach of an international obligation by both States. Where a rule of customary international law is at stake, there is no doubt that this requirement is satisfied, because both parties are bound by the same obligation. In the case of treaty law, however, "this element may limit the scope of the rule",[37] for example, where the assisted State is party to a human rights treaty and the assisting one is not.

A much disputed question is whether Article 16 refers to the *very same international obligation*, or whether it is sufficient for both States to be obliged to respect rules similar in substance, even if the source is different: for instance, in the case of two different regional treaties. The second solution appears more consistent with the principle of good faith (Article 26 of the Vienna Convention).[38]

3.2 Italy's responsibility for complicity

Before exploring whether these two requirements (i.e. the mental element and the opposability of the obligations breached) are satisfied in the present case, we can easily infer from the above-mentioned reports that Italy contributed 'significantly' to the acts of torture committed in Libya: actually, we might even conclude that in some cases the aid was essential. In fact, at least with regards to pull-backs, an active involvement of the Libyan Coast Guard in intercepting and taking migrants back to Libya would have been extremely unlikely without Italy's support, since Libya had neither the means nor the will to do so without the logistic and financial aid provided by Italy.

With regard to the mental element, I believe that, in the present case, this requirement is certainly satisfied if we abide by the text of Article 16(a) and consider 'knowledge' to be sufficient: Italy is well aware of the circumstances that render Libya's conduct internationally wrongful given that several reports have clearly demonstrated the risks for migrants in that country, plus the fact that Italy had already been condemned for the same violation by the European Court of Human Rights (ECtHR) in the *Hirsi* case. Since then, the risk of abuse of

---

36 ILC Commentary, p. 66, para. 6.
37 See Jackson, *Complicity in International Law*, cit., p. 162.
38 See Aust, cit., p. 259. See also Lanovoy, cit., p. 24.

migrants in Libya has become increasingly worse. In addition, in light of the numerous reports already available at the time of the signing of the MoU, had Italy declared (but it didn't) that it was not aware of the torture in Libya, this argument would most probably be rejected, since, as pointed out, courts usually refuse "to countenance wilful blindness to readily ascertainable facts".[39]

Conversely, if we adhere to the thesis that 'intent' is required, the interpretation given to this notion is crucial. As illustrated above, this element is mentioned only in the ILC Commentary, which however does not provide any definition. Indeed, if Article 16 (a) is interpreted as requiring a 'purpose-based test',[40] this would be difficult to achieve in the present case: there is no evidence that Italy wishes migrants in Libya to be tortured.[41] However, the view that 'intent' is to be interpreted in the sense of "awareness that wrongful acts would happen in the 'ordinary course of events'", as per international criminal law,[42] appears to be much more convincing. If we adhere to this interpretation, then the requirement is satisfied, since Italy knows that the aid provided to Libya would result in a number of migrants' human rights violations, and in particular, in torture, in the ordinary course of events.[43] Significantly, the financial, logistic and technological support provided to the Libyan border authorities is explicitly given in order to "stem the flow of migrants", i.e. to facilitate the return of migrants to Libya where they face torture and inhuman treatment. It would be another matter if aid and assistance were given in good faith – for example, for development aid – , and subsequently misused[44] by the receiving country to enforce border controls, resulting in torture and inhuman treatment. As pointed out by Agnes Callamard, Special Rapporteur of the Human Rights Council on extrajudicial, summary or arbitrary executions, "Funding initiatives to transit countries where human rights violations are endemic must be aimed at enhancing protection and must not aid or contribute to known violations in the name of migration or border control".[45]

Special Rapporteur Callamard also stated that "disregard for the human rights of migrants may trigger concerns under Articles 40 and 41

---

39 See Gammeltoft-Hansen, Hathaway, cit., p. 281.
40 See Mackenzie-Gray Scott, cit.
41 Ibidem.
42 See *supra* Moynihan, cit., p. 467 and, with specific regard to the present case, Mackenzie-Gray Scott, cit.
43 See in similar terms Mackenzie-Gray Scott, cit.
44 See in general terms Gammeltoft-Hansen, Hathaway, cit., p. 280.
45 Cit., para. 39.

of the draft articles on responsibility of States for internationally wrongful acts".[46] As explored above,[47] Article 41(2) ASR states that in case of a serious breach within the meaning of Article 40 ASR, States must not aid and assist in maintaining such a situation. Indeed, the gross violation of human rights committed in Libya may well be qualified as crimes against humanity, and fall within the scope of this article, as envisaged by the Prosecutor of the International Criminal Court, who clarified on a number of occasions that the ongoing investigations relating to Libya (following a referral by the UN Security Council) also concern "serious and widespread crimes against migrants attempting to transit through Libya".[48] Since Article 41 does not mention either knowledge or intent, Italy's complicity could also be qualified as a violation of the prohibition to aid or assist a State responsible for serious breach of human rights,[49] without the need to investigate the mental element.

Finally, the second requirement is also fulfilled in the case under examination, since there is no doubt that the torture of migrants would be considered an internationally wrongful act if committed by Italy. As we have seen *supra*,[50] it is debatable whether Article 16 means the *very same international obligation*, or if it is sufficient that both States are obliged to respect the same rule in substance, even if the source is different. In the present case, however, torture is prohibited both by a rule of customary international law and by treaties ratified by Italy and Libya (the International Covenant on Civil and Political Rights and the UN Convention against Torture).

In conclusion, there are strong arguments for affirming that Italy should be held indirectly responsible for complicity (in addition obviously to Libya's own responsibilities), although some objections have been raised.

---

46 Ibidem, para. 40.
47 See *supra*, § 3.1.1.
48 See *Statement to the United Nations Security Council on the Situation in Libya, pursuant to UNSCR 1970 (2011)* of 2 November 2018, para 15–16; of 8 May 2018, para.25–26; of 8 November 2017, para. 31; of 9 May 2017, para. 44, available at www. icc-cpi.int. See also Mann, Itamar, Moreno-Lax, Violeta, Shatz, Omer, "Time to Investigate European Agents for Crimes against Migrants in Libya", in *European Journal of International Law: Talk!*, 29 March 2018, available at https://www. ejiltalk.org/time-to-investigate-european-agents-for-crimes-against-migrants-in-libya/ (accessed on 7 October 2018).
49 De Vittor, "Responsabilità degli Stati", cit., p. 26.
50 § 3.1.2.

4 Italy's responsibility for violation of positive obligations inherent in Article 3 ECHR

As explicitly affirmed by the ILC,[1] the provision on aid and assistance analyzed in Chapter 3 may also apply in case of human rights violations, although "the concept has scarcely been acknowledged by human rights treaty monitoring bodies".[2] Conversely, human rights bodies, and in particular, the European Court of Human Rights (ECtHR), have been more willing to apply the theory of positive obligations in order to hold Member States responsible for human rights violations connected to acts committed by other States. Indeed, according to the doctrine of positive obligations, Member States are under a due diligence obligation to do all they can in order to prevent[3] human rights[4] violations by others (both private parties and other States).[5] As pointed out,[6] "positive obligations and obligations of prevention may also prove to be viable functional alternatives to

---

1 ILC Commentary, p. 67, para. 9.
2 Den Heijer, *Europe and Extraterritorial Asylum*, cit., p. 98.
3 On *due diligence* obligations of prevention, see, most recently, Forlati, Serena, "Le contenu des obligations primaires de diligence: prévention, cessation, repression ...?", in *Le standard de due diligence et la responsabilité internationale-Journée d'études franco-italienne du Mans* (S. Cassella ed), Paris, Pedone, 2018, p. 39 ff., and literature quoted therein.
4 On positive obligations inherent in human rights, see *ex multis* Pisillo Mazzeschi, Riccardo, "Responsabilité de l'État pour violation des obligations positives relatives aux droits de l'homme", in *Recueil des Cours de l'Académie de Droit International de La Haye*, Vol. 333, 2008, Leiden/Boston, Martinus Nijhoff Publishers, 2009, p. 175 ff.
5 Xenos, Dimitris, *The Positive Obligations of the State under the European Convention of Human Rights*, London/ New York, Routledge, 2012, p. 19.
6 See Aust, cit., p. 403; see also Cerone, John, "Re-examining International Responsibility: "Complicity" in the Context of Human Rights Violations", in *ILSA Journal of International and Comparative Law*, Vol. 14, N. 2, 2008, p. 532–533, available at https://nsuworks.nova.edu/cgi/viewcontent.cgi?article=1625&context=ilsajournal/ (accessed on 7 October 2018).

Article 16 ASR which may in some cases make it easier to establish the responsibility of a complicit State".

4.1 Overlap between complicity and positive obligations

We can refer to the ICJ *Bosnian Genocide* case as a strong precedent regarding the possibility of "overlapping functions of the two categories"[7]: in this case, the ICJ found that the Federal Republic of Yugoslavia failed to comply with its obligation to prevent genocide. Before coming to this conclusion, the Court had affirmed that the notion of 'due diligence' calls for an assessment *in concreto*, evoking various parameters to this end, stating that:

> "The first, which varies greatly from one State to another, is clearly the capacity to influence effectively the action of persons likely to commit, or already committing, genocide. This capacity itself depends, among other things, on the geographical distance of the State concerned from the scene of the events, and on the strength of the political links, as well as links of all other kinds, between the authorities of that State and the main actors in the events".[8]

The Court then pointed out that

> the FRY was in a position of influence over the Bosnian Serbs ... owing to the strength of the political, military and financial links between the FRY on the one hand and the Republika Srpska and the VRS on the other[9]

concluding that

> In view of their undeniable influence and of the information, voicing serious concern, in their possession, the Yugoslav federal authorities should, in the view of the Court, have made the best efforts within their power to try and prevent the tragic events then taking shape, whose scale, though it could not have been foreseen with certainty, might at least have been surmised.[10]

---

7 See Aust, cit., p. 401. *Contra*, Puma, Giuseppe, *Complicità di Stati nell'illecito internazionale*, Torino, Giappichelli Editore, 2018, p. 85–99.
8 *Bosnian Genocide* Case, para. 430.
9 Ibidem, para. 434.
10 Ibidem, para. 438.

As pointed out, in the present case the Court gave great emphasis to the political and financial links between Belgrade and the Republika Srpska: however, "the same links were at issue when the Court had to determine the responsibility for complicity".[11]

That the notion of complicity and violation of the duty to prevent may be connected is further proven by the *Corfu Channel* case,[12] "the first precedent in which the ICJ established the existence of a principle of due diligence".[13] The United Kingdom, whose vessels had been damaged when passing through the Corfu Channel because of the explosion of mines, had referred repeatedly to complicity in its claim before the ICJ, as a midpoint between the stronger hypothesis – i.e. that Albania had positioned the mines itself – and the lesser one, i.e. that Albania was aware of the presence of the mines but did not alert the British vessels. Nevertheless, the complicity argument was set aside by the court because in practice it is much more difficult to establish responsibility on the ground of complicity than on the basis of a breach of due diligence obligations.[14] Regarding the first hypothesis, the Applicant State should have given evidence not only of Albania's connivance, but should have also previously identified the State committing the principal wrongdoing. This point, however, was particularly difficult to prove: because of a controversial testimony concerning the direct involvement of Yugoslavia in positioning the mines,[15] indeed "the invocation of complicity amounted to a Pandora's box".[16] In addition, even accepting the proof concerning Yugoslavia, there was an additional complexity, since the latter was not a party to the proceeding: therefore, according to the *Monetary Gold* principle, Yugoslavia could not be judged.[17] As pointed out, "the difficulties raised by the

---

11 Aust, cit., p. 402.
12 *Corfu Channel case, Judgment of 9 April 1949, I.C.J. Reports* 1949, p. 4.
13 See Corten, Olivier, Klein, Pierre, "The Limits of Complicity as a Ground for Responsibility: Lessons Learned from the Corfu Channel Case", in *The ICJ and the Evolution of International Law* (K. Bannelier, T. Christakis, S. Heathcote eds), London, Routledge, 2011, p. 314. On the question of whether *due diligence* is a principle, see Pisillo Mazzeschi, Riccardo, "Le chemin étrange de la due diligence: d'un concept mystérieux à un concept surévalué", in *Le standard de due diligence et la responsabilité internationale-Journée d'études franco-italienne du Mans* (S. Cassella ed), Paris, Pedone, 2018, p. 323 ff.
14 See Corten, Klein, cit., 324.
15 Ibidem.
16 Ibidem.
17 According to this case law, the ICJ will not deliver a judgment where the interests of a State form the 'very subject matter' of the dispute, and that State has not accepted the ICJ jurisdiction in the matter. For a critical approach to the Monetary Gold

notion of complicity (such as the absence of a third State from the proceedings, and the difficulties in proving its involvement)"[18] could be overcome by applying the notion of due diligence, thus Albania was condemned for violation of the duty to prevent, in particular, for failure to notify the presence of mines to other States.

Additional examples of the possible overlap between the two notions are provided by the European Convention on Human Rights (ECHR) case law on extraordinary renditions. In the first judgment of 13 December 2012, in the case *El-Masri v. the former Yugoslav Republic of Macedonia* [GC],[19] there is some uncertainty[20]: on the one hand, at para. 206 the European Court of Human Rights (ECtHR) states that it must assess "whether the treatment suffered by the applicant at Skopje Airport at the hands of the special CIA rendition team is *imputable* to the respondent State",[21] thus seeming to assume that complicity in acts of torture by agents of a foreign State is sufficient to attribute the conduct of those agents to the complicit State; on the other hand, at para. 211, the Court makes an explicit reference both to active facilitation and to the theory of positive obligations:

> The respondent State must be considered directly responsible for the violation of the applicant's rights under this head since its agents actively *facilitated* the treatment and then *failed to take any measures* that might have been necessary in the circumstances of the case to prevent it from occurring.[22]

---

principles, see Klein, Natalie, "Multilateral Disputes and the Doctrine of Necessary Parties in the East Timor Case", in *Yale Journal of International Law*, Vol. 21, N. 2, 1996, p. 315–316; see also the Dissenting Opinion of Judge Weeramantry in the *East Timor* case (*Portugal* v. *Australia*, *I.C.J. Reports*, 1995, p. 159).

18 Corten, Klein, cit., p. 324.

19 ECtHR, *El-Masri v. the former Yugoslav Republic of Macedonia*, judgment of 13 December 2012 [GC], applic. No. 39630/09.

20 On these ambiguities, see Nollkaemper, André, "The ECtHR Finds Macedonia Responsible in Connection with Torture by the CIA, but on What Basis?", in *European Journal of International Law: Talk!*, 24 December 2012, available at http://www.ejiltalk.org/the-ecthrfinds-macedonia-responsible-in-connection-withtorture-by-the-cia-but-on-what-basis/ (accessed on 7 October 2018) and Jackson, Miles, "Freeing *Soering*: The ECHR, State Complicity in Torture and Jurisdiction", in *European Journal of International Law*, Vol. 27, N. 3, 2016, p. 820. See also Seibert-Fohr, Anja, "From Complicity to Due Diligence: When Do States Incur Responsibility for Their Involvement in Serious International Wrongdoing?", in *German Yearbook of International Law*, Vol. 60, N. 2017, 2018, p. 668 ff.

21 Italics added.

22 Italics added.

Then, in the 2016 *Nasr and Ghali v. Italy* case ,[23] in examining the allegation of violation of Article 3 ECHR, the Court appears to be less ambiguous in identifying as a basis for Italy's responsibility the breach of a positive obligation of protection under the Convention[24]:

> Combiné avec l'article 3, l'obligation que l'article 1 de la Convention impose aux Hautes Parties contractantes de garantir à toute personne relevant de leur juridiction les droits et libertés consacrés par la Convention leur commande de prendre des mesures propres à empêcher que lesdites personnes ne soient soumises à des tortures ou à des traitements inhumains ou dégradants, même administrés par des particuliers (Z et autres c. Royaume-Uni [GC], no 29392/95, § 73, CEDH 2001V). La responsabilité de l'État peut donc se trouver engagée lorsque *les autorités n'ont pas pris de mesures raisonnables pour empêcher la matérialisation d'un risque de mauvais traitement dont elles avaient ou auraient dû avoir connaissance.*[25]

However, in the two last cases, *Al Nashiri v. Romania* (judgment of 31 May 2018, applic. No 33234/12), at para. 668, and *Husayn (Abu Zubaydah) v. Lithuania* (judgment of 31 May 2018, applic. No 46454/11), at para. 632, the Court again refers both to complicity and to failure to take reasonable steps (violation of positive obligation of prevention).

4.2 Italy's responsibility for violations of positive obligations

There is a similar overlapping in the case under examination since Italy could also be held directly responsible for violation of positive obligations inherent in Article 3 ECHR.[26] According to the approach supported by the ECtHR, States parties to the Convention have, *inter alia*, a positive duty to prevent violations and avoid conduct that

---

23 ECtHR, *Nasr and Ghali v. Italy*, judgment of 23 February 2016, applic. No. 44883/09. See, in particular, para. 283. A further confirmation is ECtHR *Al Nashiri v. Romania*, judgment of 31 May 2018, applic. No. 33234/12 (in particular, para. 677–678).

24 See, on this point, Liguori, Anna, "Extraordinary Renditions nella giurisprudenza della Corte europea dei diritti umani: il caso Abu Omar", in *Rivista di Diritto Internazionale*, Vol. 99, N. 3, 2016, p. 784 ff.

25 Para. 283. Italics added.

26 On *due diligence* obligations with regard to the Geneva Convention relating to the Status of Refugee, see Salerno, Francesco, "L'obbligo internazionale di non-refoulement dei richiedenti asilo", in *Diritti umani e diritto internazionale*, N. 4, 2010, in particular p. 509 ff.

endangers human rights, as guaranteed by the ECHR. In order to fulfil the positive obligations stemming from Article 3 ECHR, therefore, Italy should not provide Libya with support having the explicit aim of intercepting migrants at sea and returning them to Libya. By providing such support, Italy failed "to take reasonable steps to avoid a risk of ill-treatment about which they knew or ought to have known": see *ex multis* judgment of 28 March 2000, *Mahmut Kaya v. Turkey*, applic. No. 22535/93, para. 115; *Nasr and Ghali v. Italy*, cit, para. 283; *Al Nashiri v. Romania*, cit., para. 668. In *E v. United Kingdom* the Court added: "a failure to take reasonably available measures which could have had a real prospect of altering the outcome or mitigating the harm is sufficient to engage the responsibility of the State".[27] As previously mentioned, numerous international reports clearly show that migrants in Libya are subject to indefinite detention in inhuman conditions and to all sorts of abuses and violence, including the risk of indirect *refoulement* to the very countries from which they have fled because of persecutions. The duty to employ all means available so as to prevent a wrongdoing necessarily includes the prohibition of affording support to such wrongdoing: as persuasively argued, "[t]hough due diligence is usually referred to when States fail to intervene in third party abuses, it applies *a fortiori* in cases of active contributions".[28]

Resorting to the theory of positive obligations could provide a useful alternative to the notion of complicity for a number of reasons. First, because when applying the theory of positive obligations, a court does not need to take into consideration the conduct of another State; second, because the requirement of 'knowledge' provided for by Article 16 of the Draft for complicity is more difficult to meet than the requisite that the State "know or ought to know", which is sufficient in the case of positive obligations; third, and most importantly in the case under review, according to ECtHR case law on positive obligations it might be easier to meet the jurisdiction requirement, thus facilitating the search for an effective remedy and holding outsourcing States accountable.

With regard to the first point, if one subscribes to the thesis[29] that the Serraj Government-led entity can be considered as the successor of former Libya, and therefore as bound by all the human rights treaties accepted by Colonel Gaddafi (as well as by customary international law), one can assume that the violations of the prohibition of torture

27 ECtHR, *E. and Others v United Kingdom*, judgment of 26 November 2002, applic. No. 33218/96, para 99.
28 See Seibert-Fohr, cit., p. 704 and literature quoted therein at note n. 165.
29 See Focarelli, Carlo, *Trattato di diritto internazionale*, Torino, Utet, 2015, p. 425.

and inhuman treatment perpetuated by the DCIM (Directorate for Combating Illegal Migration, part of the Libyan Ministry of Interior and in charge of migrants' detention camps) can be attributed to the Serraj Government. However, since the militias outside the Serraj Government are also guilty of perpetrating atrocities, and given the complexity of the post-Gaddafi scenario, it is debatable whether (and in which cases) these actors can be considered as *de facto* or *de jure* organs of the Libyan State or as non-State actors; whether non-State actors are bound by an obligation prohibiting torture; whether complicity may apply in "State-to-non-State interactions".[30] All these doubts can be overcome if we apply the theory of positive obligations, because on that basis Italy is responsible for violation of its own obligation of prevention, irrespective of the conduct of another State (or non-State).

With respect to the second point, the debate concerning the exact meaning of the requirement of 'knowledge' provided for by Article 16 of the Draft Articles is still ongoing. This uncertainty must, to a certain extent, be attributed to the ILC itself, as the requirement is set in three different ways, as analyzed *supra*.[31] Indeed, while Article 16 requires "*knowledge of the circumstances of the internationally wrongful act*", the ILC Commentary does not only require that the assisting State be "aware of the circumstances making the conduct of the assisted State internationally wrongful", but also that the aid must be given "*with a view to facilitating*" an internationally wrongful act (at paragraph 1), adding, at paragraph 5, that a State is not responsible unless the relevant organ "*intended* ... to facilitate the occurrence of the wrongful conduct" (italics added). So far, this mental requirement has yet to receive in-depth judicial consideration. Conversely, commentators have investigated it thoroughly, focusing both on 'knowledge' and on 'intent', arguing in some cases that "the difference between the two is in practice more apparent than real".[32] With specific regard to Italy's responsibility for complicity in the case under examination, it is interesting to refer in particular to MacEnzie-Grey Scott,[33] for a triple test of the facts in light of the notion of 'knowledge', 'purpose' and 'willful blindness'. Indeed, all three notions are more difficult to prove than constructive knowledge (i.e. that the assisting State "should have known"), which is sufficient in the case of positive obligations.

---

30 For all these points, see Mackenzie-Gray Scott, cit.
31 See § 3.1.1.
32 See for this position, as well for a thorough overview of the literature concerning this topic, Moynihan, cit. p. 455 ff.
33 MacEnzie-Grey Scott, cit.

Third,

while it is counter-intuitive to assume that the requirement to find jurisdiction may be easier with respect to positive obligations than the traditional, 'negative dimension' of human rights, some paradoxical elements of the jurisprudence of the ECtHR may indeed point in this direction.[34]

These elements of ECtHR case law may in fact open the door to overcoming the obstacle of jurisdiction and consequently smooth the way to an effective remedy to human rights violations in an externalized context.

4.2.1 Jurisdiction under ECHR

Indeed, remedies constitute the Achilles' heel of externalization.[35]

In light of the US and Australian practice of externalized border controls,[36] access to effective *domestic* review is extremely problematic, owing to serious factual and legal obstacles, both vis-à-vis the outsourcing State and the intermediary countries, especially because the risk of 'blame shifting' or 'passing the buck' among the various actors is very high.

With respect to the possibility of bringing a claim against an outsourcing State before an *international* human rights body, the major hurdle is jurisdiction.

Traditionally, a State's jurisdiction, for purposes of its human rights obligations, was assumed to be limited primarily, if not exclusively, to its territory. As international human rights law has evolved, it is now accepted that a State's jurisdiction for human rights purposes can extend to persons outside its territorial limits, whenever the State exercises 'effective control' over them, or over the territory in which they are located.

---

34 Aust, cit., p. 404.
35 See Liguori, Anna, "Some Observations on the Legal Responsibility of States and International Organizations in the Extraterritorial Processing of Asylum Claims", in *Italian Yearbook of International Law*, Vol. XXV, 2016, p. 135 ff., in particular p. 152 ff.
36 See Noll, Gregor, "Visions of the Exceptional: Legal and Theoretical Issues Raised by Transit Processing Centres and Protection Zones", in *European Journal of Migration and Law*, Vol. 5, N. 3, 2003, pp. 338 ff p. 326. See also Van Berlo, Patrick, "The Protection of Asylum Seekers in Australian-Pacific Offshore Processing: The Legal Deficit of Human Rights in a Nodal Reality", in *Human Rights Law Review*, Vol. 17, N. 1, 2017, p. 33 ff.

With respect to the ECtHR case law,[37] it is worthwhile to recall an extremely relevant statement in *Issa v. Turkey*[38]

> Article 1 of the Convention cannot be interpreted so as to allow a State party to perpetrate violations of the Convention on the territory of another State, which it could not perpetrate on its own territory.

A consistent implementation of this principle should lead to a functional approach to extraterritorial jurisdiction. However, the ECtHR jurisprudence on jurisdiction is quite puzzling. In *Banković v. Belgium*[39] the Court held that the text of "Article 1 does not accommodate" an approach to a "cause-and-effect" notion of jurisdiction (vigorously denying a functional approach); in *Al-Skeini v. the United Kingdom*,[40] after reiterating that "A State's jurisdictional competence under Article 1 is primarily territorial", the Court affirmed nonetheless the existence of jurisdiction "whenever the State, through its agents, exercises control

---

37 See, *ex multis*, Gaja, Giorgio, "Article 1", in *Commentario alla Convenzione europea per la salvaguardia dei diritti dell'uomo* (Bartole, Conforti and Raimondi eds), Padova, 2001, p. 28; De Sena, Pasquale, *La nozione di giurisdizione statale nei trattati sui diritti dell'uomo*, Torino, Giappichelli editore, 2002; O'Boyle, Michael, "The European Convention on Human Rights and Extraterritorial Jurisdiction: A Comment on 'life after Bankovic'", in *Extraterritorial Application of Human Rights Treaties* (Coomans, Kamminga eds), Antwerpen, Intersentia, 2004; Lagrange, Evelyne, "L'application de la Convention de Rome à des actes accomplis par les Etats parties en dehors du territoire national", in *Revue générale de droit international public*, Vol. 112, N. 3, 2008, p. 521 ff.; Nigro, Raffaella, "The Notion of 'Jurisdiction' in Article 1: Future Scenarios for the Extra-Territorial Application of the European Convention on Human Rights", in *The Italian Yearbook of International Law* , Vol. 20, 2010, p. 11 ff.; De Sena, Pasquale, "The Notion of 'Contracting Parties' Jurisdiction' in Article 1 of the ECHR: Some Marginal Remarks on Nigro's Paper", in *The Italian Yearbook of International Law*, Vol. 20, 2010, p. 75 ff.; Milanovic, Marko, *Extraterritorial Application of Human Rights Treaties: Law, Principles, and Policy*, Oxford, Oxford University Press, 2011; Sapienza, Rosario, "Article 1", in *Commentario breve alla Convenzione europea* (S. Bartole, P. De Sena, V. Zagrebelsky eds), Padova, Cedam, 2012, p. 13 ff.

38 ECtHR, *Issa and others v. Turkey*, judgment of 16 November 2004, applic. No. 31821/96, para. 71. See, in similar terms, the UN Human Rights Committee in the case *Lopes Burgos v. Uruguay*, Par. 12.3 (UN Doc. CCPR/C/13/D/52/1979, 29 July 1981).

39 ECtHR, *Banković and others v. Belgium*, decision of 12 December 2001 [GC], applic. No. 52207/99.

40 ECtHR, *Al-Skeini and others v. the United Kingdom*, judgment of 7 July 2011 [GC], applic. No.55721/07.

and authority over an individual" (personal model) and "when, as a consequence of lawful or unlawful military action, a Contracting State exercises effective control of an area outside that national territory" (spatial model). In the *Hirsi* case, the Court recalled both judgments, and also the *Medvedyev* case, which considered that *de facto* control over a ship suffices to establish the State party's jurisdiction (even if the people on board were not transported on the French warship).[41] A more 'functional test' has been applied in only a few cases, i.e. *Xhavara v. Albania and Italy*.[42] In this decision, the Court seems to have adopted a 'cause-and-effect' approach since, with reference to a collision which took place on the high seas, it admitted implicitly the existence of Italian jurisdiction apparently because an Italian warship *caused* the sinking of a vessel carrying Albanian migrants: "La Cour note d'emblée que le naufrage du Kater I Rades a été directement provoqué par le navire de guerre italien Sibilla. Par conséquent, toute doléance sur ce point doit être considérée comme étant dirigée exclusivement contre l'Italie". The same approach

---

41 In *Medvedyev and Others v. France* (Judgment of 29 March 2010, applic. No. 3394/03), the events in question took place on board the *Winner*, a vessel flying the flag of a third State. "[W]hen they boarded the Winner, the French commando team were obliged to use their weapons to defend themselves, and subsequently kept the crew members under their exclusive guard and confined them to their cabins during the journey to France, where they arrived on 26 June 2002. The rerouting of the Winner to France, by a decision of the French authorities, was made possible by sending a tug out of Brest harbour to tow the ship back to the French port" (para. 66). This is the reason why the Court concluded that France exercised "full and exclusive control over the Winner and its crew, at least *de facto*, from the time of its interception, in a continuous and uninterrupted manner until they were tried in France" (para. 67). The *Hirsi* case was easier, because the events took place entirely on board Italian military ships. Nonetheless, the Court affirmed that "the applicants were under the continuous and exclusive *de jure* and *de facto* control of the Italian authorities" (para. 81). As observed,

> by stressing that Italy exercised not only *de jure* control (because it enjoys under the flag ship principle exclusive jurisdiction over its vessels) but also *de facto* control (because the migrants were within the factual power of the Italian authorities) over the migrants between the boarding and their transfer to Libya, the Court sends out the message that scenarios ... where migrants remain on their own vessel but are subjected to the complete control of the authorities, are also to be brought within the ambit of the Convention.

See Den Heijer, "Reflections", cit. p. 269; see also Liguori, "La Corte europea", cit., pp. 424 e 434.

42 ECtHR, *Xhavara and others v. Albania and Italy*, decision of 11 January 2001, applic. No. 39473/98.

emerges in *PAD v. Turkey*,[43] concerning the killing of Iranian citizens by a Turkish helicopter, where the Court affirmed that "it is not required to determine the exact location of the impugned events, given that the Government had already admitted that the fire discharged from the helicopters *had caused the killing* of the applicants' relatives" (italics added). Likewise, in the decision of 3 June 2008, *Andreou v. Turkey*,[44] concerning Turkish authorities positioned behind the border killing a demonstrator inside the UN-controlled area, the Court stated that "even though the applicant sustained her injuries in territory over which Turkey exercised no control, the opening of fire on the crowd from close range, which was the direct and immediate cause of those injuries, was such that the applicant must be regarded as within the jurisdiction of Turkey".

More recently, in *Jaloud v. The Netherlands*,[45] the Court declared that the applicant fell within the jurisdiction of the Netherlands because he passed through a checkpoint "manned by personnel under the command and direct supervision of a Netherlands Royal Army officer". However, this last case confirms that the Court is probably not yet ready for a notion of 'cause and effect' jurisdiction; otherwise, as pointed out,[46] "[a]ll the talk [in Jaloud] about occupation, exercise of public authority and manning checkpoints would have been quite unnecessary".

So far, given the current case law, the concept of jurisdiction as 'effective control' will be satisfied in situations where offshore migration controls entail detention and/or ill treatment by the third State of those intercepted by the outsourcing States on the high seas (*Hirsi* judgment) or removed from Europe (*Soering* jurisprudence).

4.2.2 ECHR case law on positive obligations and jurisdiction

Because the concept of jurisdiction as 'effective control' sets too high a threshold, it however risks failing in most cases of externalized controls where the State does not enjoy direct control, but only exercises some kind of influence (situations where a State is involved in a foreign territory in a less direct way, such as establishing reception facilities run by third

---

43 ECtHR, *PAD and others v. Turkey*, decision of 28 June 2007, applic. No. 60167/00.
44 ECtHR, *Andreou v. Turkey*, judgment of 27 October 2009, applic. No.45653/99.
45 ECtHR, *Jaloud v. The Netherlands*, judgment of 20 November 2014, applic. No. 47708/08.
46 See the response of A. Sari to J. Lehmann's post "The Use of Force against People Smugglers: Conflicts with Refugee Law and Human Rights Law", 22 June 2015, available at http://www.ejiltalk.org/the-use-of-force-against-people-smugglers-conflicts-with-refugee-law-and-human-rights-law/ (accessed on 30 November 2018).

parties or, as in the case under examination, signing border control agreements with third States).[47] In all such situations, according to the circumstances of the case, the theory of positive obligations could be a useful tool for holding outsourcing States responsible because in some cases the Strasbourg Court has been ready to accept a lower threshold for jurisdiction disassociated from 'effective control' in claims related to positive obligations.[48] Among the judgments in which the ECHR Court adopted such a notion of jurisdiction with respect to positive obligations, the most relevant is *Ilascu and Others v. Moldova and Russia*,[49] with respect to both Moldova's and Russia's jurisdiction.

With regard to Moldova, the Courts affirmed that:

> However, even in the absence of effective control over the Transdniestrian region, Moldova still has a positive obligation under Article 1 of the Convention to take the diplomatic, economic, judicial or other measures that it is in its power to take and are in accordance with international law to secure to the applicants the rights guaranteed by the Convention.[50]

This ruling will be reiterated in more general terms in *Manoilescu and Dubrescu v. Romania and Russia*[51] and *Treska v. Albania and Italy*.[52] As observed,[53] these cases support a conclusion that the duty to take preventive or other positive action in respect of extraterritorial human rights violations originates first and foremost from the influence a state exercises in a particular situation, i.e. the power to prevent human rights violations, "even in the absence of effective control of a territory outside its borders" (see *Treska* and *Mainolescu*, cit.), and that "the ECtHR is at the least receptive for claims relating to positive

---

47 See Den Heijer, *Europe and Extraterritorial Asylum*, cit., p. 45.
48 See Den Heijer, *Europe and Extraterritorial Asylum*, cit., p. 48; Duffy, Helen, "The Practice of Shared Responsibility in Relation to Detention and Interrogation Abroad: The 'Extraordinary Rendition' Programme", *SHARES Research Paper* 78, 2016, p. 16, available at http://www.sharesproject.nl/publication/the-practice-of-shared-responsibility-in-relation-to-detention-and-interrogation-abroad-the-extraordinary-rendition-programme/ (accessed on 7 October 2018); Aust, cit., p. 404.
49 ECtHR, *Ilascu and others v. Moldova and Russia*, judgment of 8 July 2004, applic. No 48787/99.
50 Para. 331.
51 ECtHR, *Manoilescu and Dubrescu v. Romania and Russia*, decision of 3 March 2005, applic. No 60861/00.
52 ECtHR, *Treska v. Albania and Italy*, decision of 29 June 2006, applic. No 26937/04.
53 See Den Heijer, *Europe and Extraterritorial Asylum*, cit., p. 81.

obligations in an extraterritorial setting".[54] In other words, in these decisions, the Court explicitly disregarded "the test of effective control as a precondition for the establishment of jurisdiction".[55]

Regarding Russia's jurisdiction, the Court affirmed that:

> the "MRT", set up... *with the support* of the Russian Federation,... remains under the effective authority, *or at the very least under the decisive influence*, of the Russian Federation, and in any event ... it survives by virtue of the military, economic, financial and political support given to it by the Russian Federation.[56]

concluding:

> That being so, the Court considers that there is a continuous and uninterrupted link of responsibility on the part of the Russian Federation for the applicants' fate, as the Russian Federation's policy of support for the regime and collaboration with it continued beyond 5 May 1998, and after that date the Russian Federation made no attempt to put an end to the applicants' situation brought about by its agents, and did not act to prevent the violations allegedly committed after 5 May 1998.[57]

I am aware that the *Ilascu* case differs from that one under examination, and that in *Ilascu*, there was some confusion between jurisdiction

---

54 See Den Heijer, Maarten, Lawson, Rick, "Extraterritorial Human Rights and the Concept of "Jurisdiction"", in *Global justice, State Duties: The Extraterritorial Scope of Economic, Social and Cultural Rights in International Law* (M. Langford, W. Vandenhole, M. Sheinin, W. van Genugten eds), Cambridge, Cambridge University Press, 2013, p. 188.

55 See Rozakis, Christos, "The Territorial Scope of Human Rights Obligations: The Case of the European Convention on Human Rights", in *The Status of International Treaties on Human Rights*, Strasbourg, Council of Europe Publishing, 2005, p. 70 ff.; see also Tzevelekos, Vassilis P., Katselli Proukaki, Elena, "Migrants at Sea: A Duty of Plural States to Protect (Extraterritorially)?", in *Nordic Journal of International Law*, Vol. 86, N. 4, 2017, pp. 427 ff. *Contra* Larsen, Kjetil Mujezinović, *The Human Rights Treaty Obligations of Peacekeepers*, Cambridge, Cambridge University Press, 2012, p. 220 ff. The author admits that while in *Ilascu*, the statement was made with respect to Moldova's obligations towards a region *within its borders*, in *Mainolescu* and *Treska*, it was made with regard to Russia's obligations in Romania and Italy's obligations in Albania, respectively, i.e. *extraterritorially*. However, he concludes that the statement should be considered "as a mere slip of the tongue".

56 Para. 392. Italics added.

57 Para. 393.

and responsibility.[58] Two elements, however, are particularly relevant with respect to the Italy-Libya MoU: the considerable relevance attached by the Court to the financial support enjoyed by the MRT by virtue of agreements concluded with Russia (*Ilascu*, para. 390) and the fact that also with regard to Russia, the Court lowered "the threshold of the needed control"[59]: the 'effective control' was not required as the power to influence was sufficient.

Paraphrasing para. 392 of the *Ilascu* judgment, we might say[60]:

> The Libyan policy of pull-backs, set up in February 2017 with the support of Italy, even if Libya has its own organization, remains under the decisive influence of Italy, and in any event it survives by virtue of the technical, economic, financial and political support given by Italy.

Similarly, paraphrasing para. 393, we might conclude:

> that being so, the Court considers that there is a continuous and uninterrupted link of responsibility on the part of *Italy* for the applicants' fate, as the *Italian policy of support for the pull-back operations* started with the decisive input of *Italy Libya MoU of 2 February 2017*, and after that date *Italy did not act to prevent the violations of migrants, although it knew - or should have known - the circumstances making the conduct of the assisted State internationally wrongful.*

In other words, *mutatis mutandis*, it might be argued that Italy exercises jurisdiction because of its decisive influence on Libyan activities concerning pull-backs, as Libya would never take such actions without Italy's support.[61]

In addition, there have been some decisions in which the ECtHR quickly dismissed or did not even examine objections concerning jurisdiction in extraterritorial cases. In its decision *Haydarie v. the Netherlands*,[62] for instance, concerning the refusal of a visa to a person

---

58 Milanovic, Marko, "Grand Chamber Judgment in Catan and Others", in *European Journal of International Law Talk!*, 21 October 2012, available at https://www.ejiltalk. org/grand-chamber-judgment-in-catan-and-others/ (accessed on 7 October 2018).

59 Ibidem.

60 Those parties which have been altered in the judgment are in Italics.

61 See also Moreno-Lax, Giuffré, *The Rise of Consensual Containment*, cit.

62 ECtHR, *Haydarie v. the Netherlands*, decision of 20 October 2005, applic. No. 8876/04.

living in Pakistan, even though the Court rejected the claim on the merits, it expressly dismissed the objection raised by the Netherlands that the claimant was outside its jurisdiction. Also, in *Women on Waves v. Portugal*,[63] a foreign vessel (which intended to inform Portuguese women about their reproductive rights) was prevented from entering the territorial waters of the respondent State. Portugal was found to be in breach of ECHR (in particular of Article 10 ECHR) and no jurisdictional issue was raised.

---

63 ECtHR, *Women on Waves v. Portugal*, judgment of 3 February 2009, applic. No. 31276/05.

5 Closing remarks

To date, scholars have mainly investigated Italy's responsibility for human rights violations arising as a consequence of the 2017 Italy-Libya MoU on the basis of complicity, exploring whether the requirements provided for in Article 16 of the International Law Commission (ILC) Draft Articles on the Responsibility of States are fulfilled: i.e. that the State which aids or assists (a) does so with knowledge of the circumstances of the internationally wrongful act ('mental element'); and that (b) the act would be internationally wrongful if committed by that State ('opposability'). The vast majority of commentators came to the conclusion that both conditions are met, while others have raised arguments against this thesis. After a brief analysis of complicity in general, I myself tried to verify if Italy should be held responsible as a consequence of the aid and support provided in light of the MoU. In so doing, I reached the conclusion of considering Italy responsible for complicity, confining myself, however, to the most blatant breach, the one concerning the prohibition of torture. In fact, we can argue that at least in this case, all the objections linked to the different interpretations of the mental element are irrelevant because the widespread and systematic violations of the prohibition of torture in Libya can be considered as a crime against humanity,[1] and thus fall within the scope of Article 41(2) ASR. Indeed, this article requires States not to render assistance in maintaining situations created by a serious breach of "an obligation arising under a peremptory norm of general international law"[2] (the prohibition of torture being one), without mentioning either knowledge or intent.[3]

1 See supra § 3.2.
2 Article 40 ASR. On this provision, see Picone, cit.
3 Nolte, Aust, cit., p. 16.

However, most of the arguments against Italy's complicity may be overcome if we explore responsibility on a different basis, i.e. as arising not from aid and assistance to the wrongful act but from the breach of positive obligations. Resorting to the theory of positive obligations could certainly provide a useful alternative to the notion of complicity for a number of reasons. First, because when applying the theory of positive obligations a court does not need to take into consideration the conduct of another State; second, because the requirement of 'knowledge' provided for by Article 16 of the ILC Articles on State Responsibility for complicity is more difficult to meet than the requisite that the State "know or ought to know", which is sufficient in the case of positive obligations; third, and most importantly in the case under review, according to some "paradoxical elements of the jurisprudence of the ECtHR case law"[4] on positive obligations, it might be easier to meet the jurisdiction requirement – which is the most difficult hurdle – thus facilitating the search for an effective remedy and holding outsourcing States accountable.

Furthermore, as noted,[5]

> The inclination to become more directly involved in order to achieve more control and thereby to increase the likelihood of efficacy thus often pushes States to the more interventionist end of the spectrum of cooperation-based *non-entrée*. Yet it is when a state's own personnel are deployed in aid of deterrence abroad or where joint or shared enforcement is established that legal liability becomes most clear.

This is exactly what happened between Italy and Libya. In fact, following the signing of the MoU, on 28 July 2017, Italy launched a military mission in support of Libya by providing, *inter alia*, an Italian military ship in Tripoli to aid in "maintaining, repairing and ensuring the seaworthiness of Libyan naval vessels"[6]; and in December 2017, Italy and Libya decided to create a joint coordination centre in Tripoli.[7] In many cases, as both NGO and Libyan Coast Guard boats often came to rescue migrants at approximately the same time, the Italian Maritime Coordination Centre (hereafter, IMRCC) explicitly gave 'on scene command' to

---

4 See Aust, cit., p. 404.
5 See Gammeltoft-Hansen, Hathaway, cit., p. 284.
6 See http://www.senato.it/service/PDF/PDFServer/BGT/1039135.pdf (accessed on 30 November 2018).
7 https://www.reuters.com/article/us-europe-migrants-libya/libya-and-italy-to-set-up-operations-room-to-tackle-migrant-smuggling-idUSKBN1E30L8 (accessed on 30 November 2018).

the Libyan Coast Guard even though it was aware of the fate of migrants (return to inhuman conditions and abuses in Libya, as demonstrated above), and although, in order to execute pull-backs, Libya often put migrants' lives at risk during dangerous manoeuvres at sea while ensuring that they boarded its vessels.[8] With regard to the incident of 6 November 2017,[9] on 8 May 2018 a claim was brought before the European Court of Human Rights (ECtHR) by 17 survivors against Italy "over its coordination of Libyan Coast Guard pull-backs resulting in migrant deaths and abuse".[10] In addition, as reported,[11] NGO vessels have sometimes been explicitly requested by the IMRCC to abstain from rescuing, and to wait for the Libyan Coast Guard to arrive, at great risks to migrants' lives.[12]

Indeed, the possibility of finding a jurisdictional link in keeping with the jurisprudence of the Strasbourg Court based on 'effective control' becomes easier in all those cases in which Italy is not only supporting the Libyan Coast Guard with financial aid and means, but is directly involved in search and rescue operations, the coordination of which is "operated in practice by the Italian Coast Guard, with its own vessels and with those provided to Libya". This was recently affirmed by

8 On the incidents which occurred in 2017, see Amnesty report *Libya's Dark Web of Collusion*, p. 35 ff., https://www.amnesty.org/en/documents/mde19/7561/2017/en/ (accessed on 30 November 2018).

9 A video of the incident is available at https://sea-watch.org/en/clarification-on-the-incident-of-november-6th/ (accessed on 30 November 2018).

10 http://www.glanlaw.org/single-post/2018/05/08/Legal-action-against-Italy-over-its-coordination-of-Libyan-Coast-Guard-pull-backs-resulting-in-migrant-deaths-and-abuse (accessed on 30 November 2018); the case was brought by the Global Legal Action Network (GLAN) and the Association for Juridical Studies on Immigration (ASGI), with support from the Italian non-profit Associazione Ricreativa e Culturale Italiana (ARCI) and Yale Law School's Lowenstein International Human Rights Clinic. On this claim, see Baumgärtel, Moritz, "High Risk, High Reward: Taking the Question of Italy's Involvement in Libyan 'Pullback' Policies to the European Court of Human Rights", in *European Journal of International Law: Talk!*, 14 May 2018, available at https://www.ejiltalk.org/high-risk-high-reward-taking-the-question-of-italys-involvement-in-libyan-pullback-policies-to-the-european-court-of-human-rights/ (accessed on 5 December 2018).

11 See Biondi, Paolo, "Italy Strikes Back Again: A Push-back's Firsthand Account", in *Border Criminologies*, 15 December 2017, available at https://www.law.ox.ac.uk/research-subject-groups/centre-criminology/centreborder-criminologies/blog/2017/12/new-dutch (accessed on 7 October 2018).

12 https://www.theguardian.com/world/2018/jun/29/italy-and-libya-accused-after-migrant-deaths-in-dinghy-sinking (accessed on 30 November 2018), which reports that on 29 June 2018, the crew of Proactiva Open Arms "have said that Italian officials told them to let the Libyan coastguard respond to a distress call– only to hear shortly afterward that 100 migrants were missing and feared dead in the same area".

the Catania judge for preliminary investigations (GIP) in his decision of 27 March 2018[13] with regard to the emblematic case concerning *Proactiva Open Arms*, a Spanish NGO involved in a search and rescue operation on 15 March 2018. On this occasion, the *Proactiva Open Arms* managed to rescue two vessels in distress (denominated 'SAR event 164' and 'SAR event 166'), despite threats from the Libyan Coast Guard. As reported by a Spanish journalist who was on the *Open Arms*, the captain of the Libyan Coast Guard boat ordered the *Proactiva* crew members to hand over the migrants on board, threatening to kill the crew.[14] The Spanish crew succeeded in resisting the Libyan demand, but the stand-off lasted two hours "during which the crew repeatedly informed the Italian authorities without anyone intervening".[15] With regard to a third vessel ('SAR event 165'), the Libyan Coast Guard arrived before the NGO and, after embarking all the migrants, took them back to Libya. The *Open Arms* succeeded in reaching the Italian harbour of Pozzallo but was immediately seized because the captain of the NGO was accused of "criminal association for the purpose of illegal immigration". Italy claimed that NGOs had to hand over the survivors to Libya under its NGO Code of Conduct, "disregarding that it would have amounted to *refoulement*".[16] With regard to 'SAR event 165' (i.e. when the Libyan Coast Guard managed to intervene before the NGO and to take all the migrants back to Libya), it was convincingly argued[17] that, because of the power of

13 Available at http://www.statewatch.org/news/2018/apr/it-open-arms-sequestration-judicial-order-tribunale-catania.pdf (accessed on 30 November 2018).

14 A video is available at https://www.youtube.com/watch?v=NizZTVTkRtk (accessed on 7 October 2018).

15 See http://www.statewatch.org/analyses/no-327-open-arms-seizure.pdf (accessed on 30 November 2018).

16 See Mann, Moreno-Lax, Shatz, cit.; on the code of conduct, see Ramacciotti, Martina, "Sulla utilità di un codice di condotta per le organizzazioni non governative impegnate in attività di search and rescue (SAR)", in *Rivista di diritto internazionale*, Vol. 101, N. 1, 2018, p. 213 ff.; prior to the *Open Arms* case, another NGO boat was seized, the *Jugen Rettet Iuventa*: see Saccucci, Andrea, "La giurisdizione esclusiva dello Stato della bandiera sulle imbarcazioni impegnate in operazioni di soccorso umanitario in alto mare: il caso della Iuventa", in *Rivista di diritto internazionale*, Vol. 101, N. 1, 2018, p. 223 ff.

17 De Vittor, Francesca, "Soccorso in mare e favoreggiamento dell'immigrazione irregolare: sequestro e dissequestro della nave Open Arms", in *Diritti umani e diritto internazionale*, Vol. 12, N. 2, 2018, p. 443. The author recalls the ECtHR judgment of 12 January 2012, *Kebe and Others v. Ukraine*, appl. No. n. 12552/12, concerning an Eritrean citizen on board a ship (flying a Maltese flag) who had asked to disembark and seek asylum when the ship docked in an Ukrainian harbor. However, the applicant was allowed to leave the ship and lodge an asylum claim only after the Strasbourg Court issued an interim measure to the Ukraine to this end. In considering

control explicitly exercised over the event by the Italian authorities, migrants pulled back to Libya were within Italy's jurisdiction.

As of June 2018, Libya notified IMO of its own SAR zone,[18] and Italy, with the advent of a populist government, inaugurated new controversial measures,[19] such as denying access to Italian ports[20] (first to NGO boats flying foreign flags before entering territorial waters – i.e. in the case concerning the boat *Aquarius*[21] – later even to

---

18 the complaint of the applicant concerning violation of Article 13 in conjunction with Article 3 ECHR, the ECtHR affirmed, at para. 75, that "Ukraine had jurisdiction to decide whether the first applicant should be granted leave to enter Ukraine from the moment the Ukrainian border guards embarked the vessel and met with the applicants" concluding that "he was thus within Ukraine's 'jurisdiction', for the purposes of Article 1 of the Convention, to the extent that the matter concerned his possible entry to Ukraine" (see De Vittor, "Responsabilità degli Stati", cit., p. 21). As argued by the same author if the power to decide whether or not to authorize access was sufficient to trigger jurisdiction in this case, the same principle should be applied in the case of extraterritorial procedures for authorizing access, whenever the asylum seeker risks inhuman treatments in case of denial of entry.

18 https://www.euronews.com/2018/07/06/prompted-by-eu-libya-quietly-claims-right-to-order-rescuers-to-return-fleeing-migrants (accessed on 30 November 2018).

19 Also at domestic level: see the controversial measures introduced by Law N. 132/2018, available at http://www.gazzettaufficiale.it/eli/id/2018/12/03/18G00161/sg (accessed on 5 December 2018) and concerns expressed by UN human rights experts: see Statement of 21 November 2018, available at https://www.ohchr.org/en/NewsEvents/Pages/DisplayNews.aspx?NewsID=23908&LangID=E&fbclid=IwAR03z4o0ZKo9aAJ6N-P_T0fXj4ofawRQvvOVLIXYMMDDO1kuAnZCCsKkxRY (accessed on 5 December 2018), stating *inter alia* that

> The abolition of humanitarian protection status, the exclusion of asylum seekers from access to reception centres focusing on social inclusion, and the extended duration of detention in return centres and hotspots fundamentally undermine international human rights principles, and will certainly lead to violations of international human rights law.

20 In addition, at least in one case, an Italian towboat rescued more than 100 migrants and returned them to Libya: see https://www.telegraph.co.uk/news/2018/07/31/italian-ship-accused-taking-migrants-back-libya-first-time/ (accessed on 30 November 2018).

21 The Aquarius is an NGO boat which in June 2018, after having rescued more than 200 hundreds migrants in coordination with the IMRCC, was prevented to dock in Italy and Malta, and could finally disembark the migrants rescued only eight days later in Spain (since the trip till the Spanish harbour was quite long, however, most of the migrants had to be transferred on two Italian military vessels). On this case, see Fink, Melanie, Gombeer, Kristof, Rijpma, Jorrit, "In Search of a Safe Harbour for the Aquarius: The Troubled Waters of International and EU law" in *EU Immigration and Asylum Law and Policy*, 9 July 2018, available at http://eumigrationlawblog.eu/in-search-of-a-safe-harbour-for-the-aquarius-the-troubled-waters-of-international-and-eu-law/ (accessed on 7 October 2018). According to the authors, "by instructing the Aquarius to stand by, Italy indisputably exercises some control over it. However, it is unclear whether this control is sufficient for the

the Italian Navy ship *Diciotti*),[22] which indubitably offer additional examples of situations in which Italy's jurisdiction under the European Convention on Human Rights (ECHR) might be more easily established. Although the analysis of these measures[23] falls outside the scope of the present work, the new Italian policy indubitably increases risks for people trying to reach Europe through the Mediterranean Central Route, as dramatically illustrated by the exponential growth in the percentage of deaths by sea in the second half of 2018.[24]

purposes of bringing those on the Aquarius within Italy's jurisdiction". See also Vitiello, Daniela, "Il diritto di cercare asilo ai tempi dell'Aquarius", in *SIDIBlog*, 29 June 2018, available at http://www.sidiblog.org/2018/06/29/il-diritto-di-cercare-asilo-ai-tempi-dellaquarius/ (accessed on 7 October 2018) and Papastavridis, Efthymios, "Recent Non-Entrée Policies in the Central Mediterranean and Their Legality: A New Form of Refoulement?", in *Diritti umani e diritto internazionale*, N. 3, 2018, p. 493 ff.

22 See Savino, Mario, "The Diciotti Affair: beyond the Populist Farce", in *Verfassungsblog*, 2 September 2018, available at https://verfassungsblog.de/the-diciotti-affair-beyond-the-populist-farce/ (accessed on 7 October 2018).

23 See Cataldi, Giuseppe, "Migranti nel Mediterraneo e tutela dei diritti. Alcuni casi recenti della prassi italiana", in *Quaderni di economia sociale*, N. 2, 2018, p. 33 ff., available at https://www.sr-m.it/wp-content/uploads/woocommerce_uploads/2018/11/QES_2_18.pdf (accessed on 5 December 2018).

24 https://reliefweb.int/sites/reliefweb.int/files/resources/Mediterranean%20Migrant%20Arrivals%20Reach%2010...pdf (accessed on 30 November 2018).

Part II

The 2017 Italy-Libya Memorandum of Understanding as a small part of a broader scenario

1 The externalization of EU migration policies

The Italy-Libya MoU is not an isolated case, but a small piece of a larger scenario. Over the past decades, the European Union has been implementing different strategies of externalized border controls, such as visa requirements, carrier sanctions, extraterritorial patrolling of borders, 'safe third country' procedures. The idea of externalizing border controls is not new in the European debate: what is new is the systematic recourse to this practice by multiple arrangements with third countries (first of all, Turkey, but also several African countries), exposing migrants and asylum seekers to serious human rights violations. The new approach, inaugurated by what is known as the EU-Turkey deal,[1] was presented as a strategy to solve the "migration crisis" begun in 2015. In reality, as pointed out, "the refugee crisis is first and foremost, a policy crisis".[2] Indeed, the crisis exploded not because of the number of people reaching Europe, but because of the incapability of the EU to face this crisis in an effective and integrated manner.[3]

1 On the nature of this agreement, see *Order of the General Court* of 28 February 2017, case T-192/16, *NF v. European Council* and Cannizzaro, Enzo, "Denialism as the Supreme Expression of Realism, A Quick Comment on NF v. European Council", in *European Papers*, 15 March 2017, p. 251 ff., available at http://www.europeanpapers.eu/it/system/files/pdf_version/EP_EF_2017_I_021_Enzo_Cannizzaro_4.pdf (accessed on 7 October 2018).

2 Den Heijer, Martin, Rijpma, Jorrit J., Spijkerboer, Thomas, "Coercion, Prohibition, and Great Expectations: The Continuing Failure of the Common European Asylum System", in *Common Market Law Review*, Vol. 53, 2016, p. 607 ff. See also Chetail, Vincent, "Looking beyond the Rhetoric of the Refugee Crisis: The Failed Reform of the Common European Asylum System", in *European Journal of Human Rights*, Vol. 53, 2016, p. 584 ff.

3 See also De Bruycker, Philippe, "A Happy New Year for Migration and Asylum Policy? A Critical Review of the Legal and Policy Developments in 2016 in Relation to the Crisis of the European Union", in *EU Immigration and Asylum Law and Policy*, 18 January 2017, available at http://eumigrationlawblog.eu/a-happy-new-year-for-migration-and-asylum-policy/ (accessed on 7 October 2018).

In fact, with respect to the solutions envisaged by the Agenda on Migration regarding the internal dimension, the end result was to strengthen those elements of European law and policy that had provoked the crisis in the first place, i.e. coercion towards asylum seekers, prohibition of travelling from third countries to the European Union and unrealistic expectations of what border controls can achieve.[4] As a result, the measures envisaged were ineffective and even counterproductive.[5]

With regard to the 'external dimension', as we will see in the following paragraphs, the approach was more 'effective' (with respect to the intent pursued, i.e. stemming the flow of migrants), but at a high cost in terms of respect of migrants' human rights and credibility for the European Union.

1.1 The external dimension of EU migration and asylum policy in the GAMM and in the Agenda on Migration

During the Tampere Summit of 1999, the European Union had stressed that the external dimension was a priority in order to give substance to the new migration competences included in the 1997 Treaty of Amsterdam. Through the years, the external 'volet' became more and more important, arriving "at the core of the European agenda on migration, with the EU more than ever looking for external solutions to the crisis".[6] This trend recently reached an even faster acceleration, after the EU-Turkey statement of 18 March 2016 and the European Commission Communication of 7 June 2016, establishing a new Partnership Framework with third countries under the European Agenda on Migration.[7] In this Communication the EU-Turkey deal – a doubtful deal, highly criticized from a formal and material point of view, as we will see – is emphatically welcomed as establishing "new ways to bring order into migration flows and save lives".[8] In addition, in the Commission's view, "its elements can inspire cooperation with other key

---

4 Den Heijer, Rijpma, Spijkerboer, "Coercion", cit., p. 642.
5 Morgese, Giuseppe, "Recenti iniziative dell'Unione europea per affrontare la crisi dei rifugiati", in *Diritto immigrazione e cittadinanza*, N. 3–4/2015, p. 15 ff., Caggiano, Giandonato, "Alla ricerca di un nuovo equilibrio istituzionale per la gestione degli esodi di massa: dinamiche intergovernative, condivisione delle responsabilità fra gli Stati membri e tutela dei diritti degli individui", in *Studi sull'integrazione europea*, Vol. X, 2015, p. 459 ff.
6 See De Bruycker, cit.
7 COM(2016) 385 final.
8 Ibidem, p. 2.

third countries and point to the key levers to be activated".[9] Before dealing with these most recent developments, and their disturbing involution from a right-based approach, the present paragraph intends to briefly analyze the previous framework of the Global Approach to Migration and Mobility (GAMM).

The Global Approach to Migration and Mobility was first established in 2005 as Global Approach to Migration (GAM) and renewed in 2011 with a specific reference to mobility (GAMM), the latter intended to form a framework for the EU external migration and asylum policy, coordinating EU's dialogues and cooperation with non-EU countries, entrenched in the EU's overall external action, including development cooperation. Emphatically defined as "an example of international cooperation at its best – taking account of the interests and objectives of all involved: EU, partner countries and migrants themselves",[10] it was based on a comprehensive agenda, resting on four equally important pillars:

- Improve the organization of legal migration, and foster well-managed mobility
- Prevent and combat irregular migration, and eradicate trafficking in human beings
- Maximize the development impact of migration and mobility
- Promote international protection, and enhance the external dimension of asylum.

One of the positive aspects of this initiative is the explicit indication that the GAMM should be 'migrant-centred' and that "migration governance is not about 'flows', 'stocks' and 'routes', it is about people". In addition, respect for human rights is indicated as 'a cross-cutting' priority for all pillars and there is an explicit reference to respect for the EU Charter of Fundamental Rights as a key component of EU policies on migration.

However, the concrete application of this approach brought to light some of the shortcomings that characterize the most recent developments (the EU-Turkey deal, the new partnership framework and the most recent Summit Statements and Communications): first of all, the almost exclusive focus on prevention of irregular migration. In fact, most of the incentives and initiatives were in reality aimed at persuading third countries to reinforce their border controls and

---

9 Ibidem, p. 3.
10 https://ec.europa.eu/home-affairs/what-we-do/policies/international-affairs/global-approach-to-migration_en (accessed on 30 November 2018).

readmit irregular migrants. The second aspect of this policy which anticipates the further developments is the recourse not only to official international agreements but also to such instruments as operative agreements, concluded by Frontex directly with third countries, or informal deals outside of normal proceedings for the conclusion of international agreements, excluding both political (by the European Parliament) and judicial (by the Court of Justice) control.[11]

The 'European Agenda on Migration', elaborated in response to the European migration crisis of 2015, confirms the emphasis of the EU migration policy on cooperation with third countries in the management of migration, borders and asylum but is still based on the GAMM and on readmission agreements as a central instrument of the external dimension of EU migration policy. The most significant change concerned a progressive extension of the number of people covered by these readmission agreements, i.e. not only 'nationals' of the readmitting State, but also 'third country nationals' to be readmitted to transit countries.

The focus on partnership with third countries had however already been envisaged by dialogues among the EU and African Countries, such as the Khartoum process, launched on 28 November 2014. This gathered Ministers of the 28 EU countries, plus Eritrea, Ethiopia, Somalia, South Sudan, Sudan, Djibouti, Kenya, Egypt and Tunisia, the European and African Union Commissioners in charge of migration and development, and the EU High Representative, who agreed, among other things, to,

> [w]here appropriate, on a voluntary basis and upon individual request of a country in the region, assisting the participating countries in establishing and managing reception centres, providing access to asylum processes in line with the international law, if needed, improving camp services and security, screening mixed migratory flows and counselling migrants.[12]

Particularly relevant on the matter of externalization is also the Valletta Summit of November 2015, which put migration at the heart of the EU's relations with African countries and envisaged jointly exploring "the concept of enhanced capacities in priority regions along

---

11 Art. 218 TFEU.
12 See Declaration of the Ministerial Conference of the Khartoum Process, p. 4, available at http://www.esteri.it/mae/approfondimenti/2014/20141128_political_declaration.pdf (accessed on 30 November 2018).

the main migratory routes, with a view to developing possible *pilot projects*, in cooperation with UNHCR".[13]

However, the real change of paradigm was the EU-Turkey Joint Action Plan of 29 November 2015 and even more so, the EU-Turkey statement of 18 March 2016.

1.2 The EU-Turkey statement of 18 March 2016

The turning point is the EU-Turkey Statement of 18 March 2016. In fact, this 'deal' does not concern the readmission of rejected asylum seekers and irregular migrants who are to be expelled,[14] but aims at removing both migrants and asylum seekers to a transit country (Turkey) at an early stage on the basis of a 'safe third country' concept, "despite the many doubts if Turkey can be labelled as a safe third country".[15]

The deal was made public via a press release of 18 March 2016[16] under the title "EU-Turkey Statement" which, after recalling the commitments of the Action Plan of November 2015[17] and the statement of 7 March 2016,[18] states as follows:

---

13 Valletta Summit Action Plan, p. 10, at: http://www.consilium.europa.eu/en/meetings/international-summit/2015/11/11-12 (accessed on 30 November 2018).

14 At the time of the statement, the EU-Turkey readmission agreement, concluded in May 2014 (available at https://eur-lex.europa.eu/legal-content/EN/TXT/PDF/?uri=CELEX:22014A0507(01)&from=EN treaty), had entered into force, but it applied only to Turkish citizens. This is because Turkey negotiated a three-year delay with regard to third country nationals. However, as observed, "in light of the perceived migration and refugee crisis, the EU was not willing to wait that long until it called upon Turkey to accept third-state citizens back onto its territory": see Peers, Steve, Roman, Emanuela, "The EU, Turkey and the Refugee Crisis: What Could Possibly Go Wrong?", in *EU Law Analysis*, 05 February 2016, http://eulawanalysis.blogspot.com/2016/02/the-eu-turkey-and-refugee-crisis-what.html (accessed on 30 October 2018).

15 See Strik, Tineke, "The Global Approach to Migration and Mobility", in *Groningen Journal of International Law*, Vol. 5, N. 2, 2017, p. 324, available at http://www.academia.edu/35869309/The_Global_Approach_to_Migration_and_Mobility (accessed on 7 October 2018).

16 http://www.consilium.europa.eu/en/press/press-releases/2016/03/18/eu-turkey-statement/ (accessed on 30 November 2018).

17 https://www.consilium.europa.eu/en/press/press-releases/2015/11/29/eu-turkey-meeting-statement/ (accessed on 30 November 2018).

18 https://www.consilium.europa.eu/en/press/press-releases/2016/03/08/eu-turkey-meeting-statement/ (accessed on 30 November 2018). For an overview of the background of the Statement of 18 March 201, see Peers, Roman, "The EU, Turkey and the Refugee Crisis", cit.

The EU and Turkey today decided to end the irregular migration from Turkey to the EU. In order to achieve this goal, they agreed on the following additional action points:

1   All new irregular migrants crossing from Turkey into Greek islands as from 20 March 2016 will be returned to Turkey. This will take place in full accordance with EU and international law, thus excluding any kind of collective expulsion. All migrants will be protected in accordance with the relevant international standards and in respect of the principle of *non-refoulement*. It will be a temporary and extraordinary measure which is necessary to end the human suffering and restore public order. Migrants arriving in the Greek islands will be duly registered and any application for asylum will be processed individually by the Greek authorities in accordance with the Asylum Procedures Directive, in cooperation with UNHCR. Migrants not applying for asylum or whose application has been found unfounded or inadmissible in accordance with the said directive will be returned to Turkey. Turkey and Greece, assisted by EU institutions and agencies, will take the necessary steps and agree to any necessary bilateral arrangements, including the presence of Turkish officials on Greek islands and Greek officials in Turkey as from 20 March 2016, to ensure liaison and thereby facilitate the smooth functioning of these arrangements. The costs of the return operations of irregular migrants will be covered by the EU.

2   For every Syrian being returned to Turkey from Greek islands, another Syrian will be resettled from Turkey to the EU taking into account the UN Vulnerability Criteria. A mechanism will be established, with the assistance of the Commission, EU agencies and other Member States, as well as the UNHCR, to ensure that this principle will be implemented as from the same day the returns start. Priority will be given to migrants who have not previously entered or tried to enter the EU irregularly.

As counterpart for Turkey, the Statement provides for acceleration of the fulfilment of the visa liberalization process concerning Turkish citizens, upgrading of the Customs Union, disbursement of €3 billion (and the promise of an additional €3 billion by the end of 2018) and the commitment "to re-energise the accession process".[19]

Many criticisms were raised since the very beginning, all based on two differing points of view: one concerning human rights issues, another based on European constitutional law, regarding *inter alia* whether it was an agreement or a non-binding political arrangement. Since the legal nature of the Statement remains controversial, as we will see in para. 1.2.2, we will use both the expressions 'statement' and 'deal' interchangeably.

1.2.1 Criticism concerning human rights and refugee law

As pointed out,[20] the first sentence of the deal "is a flagrant breach of EU and international law – but the rest of the paragraph then completely contradicts it". On the one hand, sending back 'all' persons crossing from Turkey to the Greek islands would violate the prohibition of collective expulsion provided for in the EU Charter and the European Convention on Human Rights (ECHR), as well as EU asylum legislation. On the other hand, the reference to the relevant international standards and to the principle of *non-refoulement,* together with the explicit provision for individual assessment, indicate that this should not be the case. The Statement adds that "Migrants not applying for asylum or whose application has been found unfounded or inadmissible in accordance with the said directive will be returned to Turkey". This means that it will also be possible to send back people in need of protection whose claims are considered 'inadmissible' (without examination of the merits), on the grounds that Turkey is either a 'safe third country' or a 'first country of asylum'. In other words, applications "would not be rejected on the basis that the person *wasn't a genuine refugee*, but that he or she either (a) *could have* applied for protection in Turkey[21]

---

19 The EU-Turkey Statement, par. 8.

20 Peers, Steve, "The Final EU/Turkey Refugee Deal: A Legal Assessment", in *EU Law Analysis*, 18 March 2016, available at http://eulawanalysis.blogspot.com/2016/03/the-final-euturkey-refugee-deal-legal.html (accessed on 30 October 2018).

21 According to Article 38(1) of the Asylum Procedures Directive, a third country can be considered 'safe' for asylum seekers if in the third country concerned:

(a) life and liberty are not threatened on account of race, religion, nationality, membership of a particular social group or political opinion;

(b) there is no risk of serious harm as defined in Directive 2011/95/EU;

(c) the principle of *non-refoulement* in accordance with the Geneva Convention is respected;

['Safe third country' concept] or (b) already *had* protection there" ['First country of asylum' concept].[22, 23]
A number of concerns have been raised.[24] First of all, we must point out that, though Turkey is a member of the Geneva Convention, it

---

(d) the prohibition of removal, in violation of the right to freedom from torture and cruel, inhuman or degrading treatment as laid down in international law, is respected; and
(e) the possibility exists to request refugee status and, if found to be a refugee, to receive protection in accordance with the Geneva Convention.

22 According to Article 35 a third country can be a first country of asylum in two cases:

a) if the applicant has been recognized as a refugee in that country and can still avail himself or herself of that protection; or
b) if the applicant otherwise enjoys sufficient protection in that country, including benefiting from the principle of *non-refoulement*.

23 Peers, Roman, "The EU, Turkey and the Refugee Crisis", cit.
24 On the EU-Turkey Statement see also: Roman, Emanuela, *L'accordo UE-Turchia: le criticità di un accordo a tutti i costi*, in *SIDIBlog*, 21 March 2016, available at http://www.sidiblog.org/2016/03/21/laccordo-ueturchia-le-criticita-di-un-accordo-a-tutti-i-costi/ (accessed on 7 October 2018); Den Heijer, Martin, Spijkerboer, Thomas, "Is the EU-Turkey Refugee and Migration Deal a Treaty?", in *EU Law Analysis*, 7 April 2016, available at http://eulawanalysis.blogspot.be/2016/04/is-eu-turkey-ref-ugee-and-migration-deal.html (accessed on 7 October 2018); Labayle, Henri, De Bruycker, Philippe, "L'accord Union européenne-Turquie: faux semblant ou marché dedupes?", in *Réseau Universitaire européen du droit de l'Espace de liberté, sécurité et justice*, 23 March 2016, available at http://www.gdr-elsj.eu/2016/03/23/asile/laccord-union-europeenne-turquie-faux-semblant-ou-marche-de-dupes/ (accessed on 7 October 2018); Favilli, Chiara, "La cooperazione UE-Turchia per contenere il flusso dei migranti e richiedenti asilo: obiettivo riuscito?", in *Diritti umani e diritto internazionale*, Vol. 10, N. 2,2016, p. 405 ff.; Fernández Arribas, Gloria, "The EU-Turkey Agreement: A Controversial Attempt at Patching up a Major Problem", in *European Papers*, 2016, available at http://europeanpapers.eu/en/system/files/pdf_version/EP_EF_2016_I_040_Gloria_Fernandez_Arribas_2.pdf (accessed on 7 October 2018); Corten, Olivier, Dony, Marianne, "Accord politique ou juridique: quelle est la nature du "machin" conclu entre l'UE et la Turquie en matière d'asile?", in *EU Immigration and Asylum Law and Policy*, 10 June 2016, http://eumigrationlaw blog.eu/accord-politique-ou-juridique-quelle-est-la-nature-du-machin-conclu-entre-lue-et-la-turquie-en-matiere-dasile/ (accessed on 7 October 2018); Cherubini, Francesco, "The 'EU-Turkey Statement' of 18 March 2016: A (Umpteenth?) Celebration of Migration Outsourcing", in *Europe of Migrations: Policies, Legal Issues and Experiences* (S. Baldin, M. Zago eds), Trieste, EUT Edizioni Università di Trieste, 2017, p. 32 ff.; Marchegiani, Maura, Marotti, Loris, "L'accordo tra l'Unione europea e la Turchia per la gestione dei flussi migratori: cronaca di una morte annunciata", in *Diritto, Immigrazione e Cittadinanza*, N. 1-2/2016, p. 59 ff.; Rizzo, Alfredo, "La dimensione esterna dello spazio di libertà, sicurezza e giustizia. Sviluppi recenti e sfide aperte", in *Freedom, Security & Justice: European Legal Studies*, N. 1, 2017, p. 147 ff., available at http://www.fsjeurostudies.eu/files/2017.1.-FSJ_Rizzo_8.pdf, (accessed on 7 October 2018).

maintains the geographical limitation, applying the Convention only to European refugees. Non-European asylum seekers enjoy a form of temporary protection, which is stronger for Syrians, but at the time of the Declaration, significantly less important than the one recognized under the Geneva Convention. Turkey however agreed to modify some of the most critical aspects of the protection enjoyed by Syrians and actually intervened on two crucial points of the legislation concerning Syrians, allowing those who had left Turkey not to lose protection once they were sent back to Turkey and to have access to the labour market there.[25]

In light of these changes, Turkey could, in abstract, qualify as 'a first country of asylum'[26] for those Syrians who already enjoyed protection in Turkey and reached Greece. But can Turkey be considered 'a safe third country' for all the other asylum seekers? This is a much debated question. According to Article 38 par. 1, e) "the possibility shall exist for the applicant to claim refugee status and to receive protection in accordance with the Geneva Convention". UNHCR's interpretation is that "access to refugee status and to the rights of the 1951 Convention must be ensured in law, including ratification of the 1951 Convention and/or the 1967 Protocol, and in practice".[27] This interpretation is supported by two arguments, as convincingly argued[28]: the legislative history of the text and the *a contrario* rule. With regard to the first argument, the 2002 draft explicitly stated that the clause could apply if a State had not ratified the Convention. However, the text was later revised to its current version and the effort of some Member States to introduce the provision that alternative forms of protection were sufficient failed. With respect to the second argument, when the drafters of the Directive wanted to provide the possibility of applying for an alternative form of protection, they did so explicitly, as in Article. 35 for the "first country of asylum" notion.[29] However, the real prob-

25 See COM(2016) 231 final, *First Report on the progress made in the implementation of the EU-Turkey Statement*, p. 4.

26 See Favilli, "La cooperazione UE-Turchia", cit., p. 415.

27 See UNHCR Paper of 23 March 2016, *Legal considerations on the return of asylum-seekers and refugees from Greece to Turkey as part of the EU-Turkey Cooperation in Tackling the Migration Crisis under the safe third country and first country of asylum concept,* available at http://www.unhcr.org/56f3ec5a9.pdf (accessed on 7 October 2018).

28 See Peers, Roman, "The EU, Turkey and the Refugee Crisis", cit.

29 Ibidem. See also Favilli, "La cooperazione UE-Turchia", cit., p. 415. See *contra* Thym, Daniel, "Why the EU-Turkey Deal is Legal and a Step in the Right Direction" in *Verfassungsblog*, 9 March 2016, available at https://verfassungsblog.de/why-the-eu-turkey-deal-is-legal-and-a-step-in-the-right-direction/ (accessed on 7 October 2018).

lem lies in the respect of human rights in practice,[30] especially because of the harsh conditions of detention[31] and the risk of *refoulement*, at least in some cases.[32] Serious human rights violations were also denounced in 2017 and 2018: Human Rights Watch attested that Istanbul and eight other provinces near the Syrian border "suspended registration for newly arriving Syrians since late 2017 or early 2018"[33] and that "Turkish security forces have routinely intercepted hundreds, and at times thousands, of asylum seekers at the Turkey-Syria border since at least December 2017 and summarily deported them to the war-ravaged Idlib governorate in Syria"[34].

Indeed, the respect of asylum seekers' human rights in Turkey is not the only concern: as recognized explicitly in the Statement of 18 March 2018, individual assessment is needed and it is up to Greece to accomplish this task. This is very problematic in light of the systematic violations of asylum seekers' rights in Greece,

---

30 See *inter alia* the "DCR/ECRE desk research on application of a safe third country and a first country of asylum concepts to Turkey" of May 2016, available at https://www.ecre.org/desk-research-on-the-application-of-the-safe-third-country-and-first-country-of-asylum-concepts-to-turkey/ (accessed on 7 October 2018); Jesuit Refugee Service European Policy Discussion Paper, "The EU-Turkey Deal", 2016, available at https://jrseurope.org/assets/Publications/File/JRS_Europe_EU_Turkey_Deal_policy_analysis_2016-04-30.pdf (accessed on 7 October 2018); Report from GUE/NGL Delegation to Turkey "What Merkel, Tusk and Timmermans should have seen during their visit to Turkey", 2–4 May 2016, available at www.europarl.eu (accessed on 7 October 2018).

31 As observed, "Turkey has a record of treating asylum-seekers and refugees harshly in detention: episodes of torture or inhuman or degrading treatment have been reported by NGOs (Global Detention Project and Amnesty International among others) and condemned by the ECtHR in a series of judgments (see for instance, *Abdolkhani and Karimnia v Turkey* and the recent *SA v Turkey*, judgement of 15 December 2015)": see Peers, Roman, "The EU, Turkey and the Refugee Crisis", cit.

32 Several reports attest of *refoulement* practices by Turkey: see, in particular, the reports from Human Rights Watch of November 2015 (https://www.hrw.org/news/2015/11/23/turkey-syrians-pushed-back-border), and Amnesty International of December 2015 (https://www.amnesty.org/en/documents/eur44/3022/2015/en/), denouncing push-backs and physical violence against migrants trying to cross the Turkish southern border coming from Syria or Iraq.

33 https://www.hrw.org/news/2018/07/16/turkey-stops-registering-syrian-asylum-seekers (accessed on 30 October 2018).

34 https://www.hrw.org/news/2018/03/22/turkey-mass-deportations-syrians (accessed on 30 October 2018). In October 2018 a report from *The Guardian* attested that Syrians trying cross the Turkish border are "invited" to sign a waiver to their right to asylum or threatened of indefinite detention: https://www.theguardian.com/global-development/2018/oct/16/syrian-refugees-deported-from-turkey-back-to-war?CMP=share_btn_tw (accessed on 30 October 2018).

as acknowledged by the Court of Strasbourg in several judgments condemning directly Greece (for the condition of detention and violation of the procedural rights of asylum seekers) and indirectly countries that wanted to send people back there in application of the Dublin regulation[35] (from the well-known ECtHR judgment *M.S.S. v. Belgium and Greece*[36] onwards, followed by the CJEU judgment N.S.).[37] Following implementation of the statement, the situation became increasingly worse with regard to reception conditions. As recently denounced

> Subsequent to the implementation of the EU-Turkey statement, Greek *hotspots* have now become places of *de facto* detention, where fast-track asylum and return procedures are being carried out with the aim of achieving an expedited return of asylum seekers to Turkey.[38]

In spite of this, the first claim, in the case *J.R. and others v. Greece*[39] concerning the circumstances and the conditions of detention of three

35 See *ex multis* Peers, Steve, "The Dublin III Regulation", in *EU Immigration and Asylum Law* (S. Peers, V. Moreno-Lax, M. Garlick, E. Guild eds), Vol. 3, 2nd Ed., Leiden/Boston, Brill–Nijhoff, 2015, p. 345 ff.; Nascimbene, Bruno, "Refugees, the European Union and the 'Dublin System'. The Reasons for a Crisis", in *European Papers*, 2016, p. 101 ff., available at http://europeanpapers.eu/it/e-journal/refugees-european-union-and-dublin-system-reasons-crisis (accessed on 15 November 2018) and most recently, Di Filippo, Marcello, "The Allocation of Competence in Asylum Procedures under EU law: The Need to Take the Dublin Bull by the Horns", in *Revista de Derecho Comunitario Europeo*, Vol. 22, N. 59, April 2018, p. 41 ff.

36 ECtHR, *M.S.S. v. Belgium and Greece*, judgment of 21 January 2011 [GC], applic. No. 30696/09.

37 See CJEU, judgment of 21 December 2011, joined cases, *N. S. v Secretary of State for the Home Department*, case C-411/10 and *M. E. and Others v Refugee Applications Commissioner and Minister for Justice, Equality and Law Reform*, case C-493/10.

38 https://www.tni.org/en/publication/expanding-the-fortress (accessed on 30 November 2018).

39 ECtHR, *J. R. and others v. Greece*, judgment of 25 January 2018, applic. No. 22696/16. On this case, see Gatta, Francesco Luigi, "Detention of Migrants with the View to Implement the EU-Turkey Statement: the Court of Strasbourg (Un)Involved in the EU Migration Policy", in *Cahiers de l'EDEM*, 2018, available at https://uclouvain.be/fr/instituts-recherche/juri/cedie/actualites/judgment-of-the-european-court-of-human-rights-in-the-case-j-r-and-others-v-greece-appl-no-22696-16.html (accessed on 7 October 2018) and Pijnenburg, Annick, "JR and Others v Greece: What Does the Court (Not) Say About the EU-Turkey Statement?", in *Strasbourg Observer*, available at https://strasbourgobservers.com/2018/02/21/

Afghan nationals in the Greek hotspot on the island of Chios as a consequence of the implementation of the EU-Turkey statement, was rejected
by the Strasbourg Court in its judgment of 25 January 2018 with regard
to the complaint lodged under Article 5 para. 1 (f) and under Article 3
ECHR (only the claim concerning Article 5 para. 2 was upheld, as the applicants were not accurately informed of the reasons for their deprivation
of liberty nor of the available legal remedies).[40] With regard to the complaint as per Article 5 para. 1 (f), the Strasbourg Court first had to decide
if keeping migrants in the hotspots could be deemed 'detention', at least
with respect to the first period of the applicants' stay in the centre (from
21 March to 20 April 2016), when it was a closed facility: from 21 April
2016 the Chios hotspot became a semi-open centre, where the applicants
could move about during the day (while still subjected to a restriction
of movement: i.e. leaving the island was forbidden).[41] On the merits, the
Court affirmed that the one-month period of detention on the island of
Chios could not be considered as arbitrary and unlawful as it

> avait pour but de les empêcher de séjourner de façon irrégulière
> sur le territoire grec, de garantir leur éventuelle expulsion, et de les
> identifier et de les enregistrer dans le cadre de la mise en œuvre de
> la Déclaration UE-Turquie.[42]

As pointed out, the judgment can be considered "as a sort of endorsement of the EU-Turkey Statement insofar as its implementation con-
stitutes, under certain conditions, a legitimate reason for the detention
of migrants".[43] The most critical part of the decision, however, is the
part that deals with the complaint as per Article 3 ECHR. As stated
in the Grand Chamber judgment in the *Khlaifia* case,[44] the Court

---

jr-and-others-v-greece-what-does-the-court-not-say-about-the-eu-turkey-
statement/ (accessed on 7 October 2018).

40 Indeed the Greek government provided them with leaflets, but according to the
ECtHR, the information was not sufficiently clear and comprehensible for the
applicants.

41 On the restriction of asylum seekers' freedom of movement, see Ziebritzki, Catharina,
Nestler, Robert, "Implementation of the EU-Turkey Statement: EU Hotspots
and Restriction of Asylum Seekers' Freedom of Movement", in *EU Immigration
and Asylum Law and Policy*, 22 June 2018, available at http://eumigrationlawblog.
eu/implementation-of-the-eu-turkey-statement-eu-hotspots-and-restriction-of-
asylum-seekers-freedom-of-movement/ (accessed on 5 December 2018).

42 ECtHR, *J.R. and others v. Greece*, cit., par. 112.

43 Gatta, cit.

44 ECtHR, *Khlaifia and others v. Italy*, judgment of 15 December 2016 [GC], applic.
No. 16483/12.

acknowledges that "la Grèce a connu une augmentation exceptionnelle et brutale des flux migratoires" and comes to the conclusion that the conditions were not severe enough to be qualified as inhuman or degrading, although governmental and non-governmental organizations attest to dramatic conditions of physical violence, and lack of legal advice and adequate health care in Greek hotspots.

Particularly interesting to this end are the Resolution adopted by the Parliamentary Assembly of the Council of Europe on 20 April 2016[45]; the Preliminary observations made by the delegation of the European Committee for the Prevention of Torture and Inhuman or Degrading Treatment or Punishment (CPT) of the Council of Europe, issued after a visit to Greece in April 2018[46]; the *Médicin Sans Frontières* Report of July 2018[47]; the UNHCR press release of 31 August 2018[48]; the Joint NGO Statement (concerning the reception conditions on the North Aegean Islands) of 13 September 2018[49]; the report of the Commissioner for Human Rights of the Council of Europe, Dunja Mijatović, released on 6 November 2018 following a visit to Greece that had taken place in June 2018.[50]

There are however other cases pending (for instance, the case *Allaa KAAK and others v. Greece*, applic. No. 34215/16, communicated to the government on 7 September 2017) and hopefully the Court will take a more courageous position.[51]

45 Resolution 2109 (2016), available at http://assembly.coe.int/nw/xml/XRef/Xref-XML2HTML-en.asp?fileid=22738&lang=en (accessed on 30 October 2018).

46 http://www.statewatch.org/news/2018/jun/coe-cpt-greece-prelim-report.pdf (accessed on 30 November 2018).

47 https://www.msf.org/confinement-violence-and-chaos-how-european-refugee-camp-traumatising-people-lesbos(accessed on 30 October 2018). With regard to Lesbos (Moira facility) – hosting three times more asylum seekers than its official capacity – see the letter sent to the European Commission by 12 NGOs: http://www.refucomm.com/includes/pdf/human-rights/open-letter_chios_european-commission_august-2018.pdf.

48 http://www.unhcr.org/news/briefing/2018/8/5b88f5c34/unhcr-urges-greece-address-overcrowded-reception-centres-aegean-islands.html (accessed on 30 November 2018).

49 https://reliefweb.int/report/greece/joint-ngo-statement-conditions-north-aegean-islands-conditions-moria-are-shameful-enel (accessed on 30 November 2018).

50 CommDH(2018)24, available at https://rm.coe.int/report-on-the-visit-to-greece-from-25-to-29-june-2018-by-dunja-mijatov/16808ea5bd?utm_source=ECRE+Newsletters&utm_campaign=ad2e4a67de-EMAIL_CAMPAIGN_2018_11_16_11_35&utm_medium=email&utm_term=0_3ec9497afd-ad2e4a67de-420537749 (accessed on 16 November 2018).

51 With regard to the responsibility of European States for human rights violations in hotspot, see Casolari, Federico, "The EU's Hotspot Approach to Managing the Migration Crisis: A Blind Spot for International Responsibility?", in *The Italian Yearbook of International Law*, Vol. 25, 2016, p.109 ff. With regard, in particular,

1.2.2 Criticism concerning European Constitutional law

The Statement has also been criticized for being concluded without respecting the constitutional requirements set by the Treaty on the Functioning of the EU (hereafter, TFEU), in particular, for not having been submitted either to the European Parliament for approval (218(6) TFEU)[52] or to the preventive control of the Court of Justice (Article 218(11) TFEU).

Indeed, a debate arose in literature regarding the legal nature of the Statement.[53] The position of EU institutions on the matter was characterized by ambiguities and *revirements*. On 18 March 2016, the same day of the adoption of the EU-Turkey Statement, the President of the European Council, Donald Tusk, affirmed that "Today, we have finally reached an agreement between the EU and Turkey"[54]; during a debate held within the European Parliament on 13 April 2016, both the President of the European Council, Donald Tusk, and the President of the European Commission, Jean-Claude Juncker, referred to the

---

to minors detained in hotspot, a claim is pending against Italy: see *Alagie Trawalli and Others v. Italy*, Appl. 47287/17, communicated to the government on 11 January 2018.

52 The Lisbon Treaty strengthened the role of the European Parliament also in relation to EU international agreements, providing that in any case "the European Parliament shall be immediately and fully informed at all stages of the procedure" (Art. 218 para. 10) and that in a number of cases, approval is needed (Art. 218 para.6). Among these last cases, also the hypothesis of agreement "covering fields to which the ordinary legislative procedure applies", which is the case of the EU-Turkey deal.

53 Among scholars arguing that it is a treaty, see Den Heijer, Martin, Spijkerboer, Thomas, "Is the EU-Turkey refugee", cit.; Corten, Olivier, Dony, Marianne, cit.; Cannizzaro, Enzo, "Disintegration Through Law?", in *European Papers*, 2016, p. 3 ff., available at Shttp://europeanpapers.eu/en/system/files/pdf_version/EP_eJ_2016_1_2_Editorial_EC.pdf (accessed on 7 October 2018); Fernández Arribas, Gloria, "The EU-Turkey Statement, the Treaty-Making Process and Competent Organs. Is the Statement an International Agreement?", in *European Papers*, 2017, p. 309, available at http://www.europeanpapers.eu/fr/system/files/pdf_version/EP_EF_2017_I_012_Gloria_Fernandez_Arribas_1.pdf (accessed on 7 October 2018). *Contra* Peers, Steve, "The Draft EU/Turkey Deal on Migration and Refugees: Is It Legal?", *EU Law Analysis*, 16 March 2016, available at http://eulawanalysis.blogspot.be/2016/03/the-draft-euturkey-deal-on-migration.html (accessed on 30 October 2018).

54 European Council, "Remarks by President Donald Tusk after the meeting of the EU heads of state or government with Turkey", 18 March 2016, http://www.consilium.europa.eu/en/press/press-releases/2016/03/18/tusk-remarks-after-euco-turkey/ (accessed on 30 November 2018).

statement as a 'deal' between the European Union and Turkey[55]; on 20 April 2016, the Commission issued a press release in which it referred to the EU-Turkey Statement as the "*EU-Turkey Agreement*.[56] However, revirements occurred in the following weeks: during a debate in the European Parliament on 28 April 2016, the President-in-Office of the Council, Klaas Dijkhoff, referred to it as "*a political agreement between the Member States and Turkey – between Europe and Turkey – ...*"[57]; on 9 May 2016, the legal service of the European Parliament stated that the EU-Turkey Statement "*was nothing more than a press communiqué*"; finally, in its controversial order of 28 February 2017, the General Court – called to solve the matter of the legal nature of the statement in three joined cases, *NF, NG and NM v. European Council* (cases T-192/16, T-193/16, T-257/16) – issued no decision as to whether the EU-Turkey statement is a political arrangement or a legally binding treaty in the sense of Articles 216–218 TFEU and dismissed the claim for lack of jurisdiction, stating that the statement was concluded by the Member States and not by the EU:

> [I]independently of whether it constitutes, as maintained by the European Council, the Council and the Commission, a political statement or, on the contrary, as the applicant submits, a measure capable of producing binding legal effects, the EU-Turkey statement, as published by means of Press Release No 144/16, cannot be regarded as a measure adopted by the European Council, or, moreover, by any other institution, body, office or agency of the European Union.

An appeal was lodged before the Court of Justice, which by an order of 12 September 2018, dismissed it without taking a position on this point. Before going through both orders (in the next chapter), it is noteworthy to recall that in the above-mentioned judgment of 25 January 2018

55 European Parliament, "Minutes of the debate of Wednesday 13 April 2016", 13 April 2016, http://www.europarl.europa.eu/sides/getDoc.do?type=CRE&reference=20160413&secondRef=ITEM-005&language=EN (accessed on 30 November 2018).

56 European Commission, "Implementing the EU-Turkey Agreement – Questions and Answers", 20 April 2016, http://europa.eu/rapid/press-release_MEMO-16-1494_en.htm (accessed on 30 November 2018).

57 European Parliament, "Minutes of the debate of Thursday 28 April 2016", 28 April 2016, http://www.europarl.europa.eu/sides/getDoc.do?pubRef=-%2f%2fEP%2f%2fTEXT%2bCRE%2b20160428%2bITEM-002%2bDOC%2bXML%2bV0%2f%2fEN&language=EN (accessed on 30 November 2018).

regarding the case *J.R. and others v. Greece,* the European Court of Human rights (ECtHR) aligned itself with the EU courts with regard to the question of attribution, but did not take a clear position on the legal nature of the statement: indeed, at para. 7, it refers to the Statement as "un *accord*[58] sur l'immigration conclu le 18 mars 2016 entre les États membres de l'Union européenne et la Turquie", while at para. 39, it states that "Le 18 mars 2016, les membres du Conseil européen et le gouvernement turc se sont entendus sur une *déclaration*[59] visant à lutter contre les migrations irrégulières".

The EU-Turkey statement is not, however, an isolated case: also in the EU-Afghanistan 'Joint Way Forward on migration issues', the Commission has clearly affirmed that the text is not binding although its wording is very similar to formal readmission agreements concluded so far by the European Union.[60]

1.3 From the European Commission communication of 7 June 2016 establishing a new Partnership Framework with third countries to the European Council conclusions of 28 June and 18 October 2018

Despite the numerous criticisms that emerged from the very beginning regarding the EU-Turkey statement, on 7 June 2016, the Commission adopted a Communication establishing a new Migration Partnership Framework with third countries[61] (hereafter, MPF) – endorsed by the European Council of 28 June 2016[62] – which explicitly intended to reproduce the EU-Turkey deal, described as a source of inspiration[63] and as a model of effectiveness.[64]

As pointed out, "The self-declared objective of the MPF is to develop win-win relationships with third country partners to better manage

---

58 Italics added.
59 Italics added.
60 Limone, Luigi, "EU-Afghanistan 'Joint Way Forward on Migration Issues': Another 'Surrealist' EU Legal Text?", in *European Area of Freedom, Security & Justice*, 11 April 2017, available at https://free-group.eu/2017/04/11/euafghanistan-joint-way-forward-on-migration-issues-anothersurrealist-eu-legal-text/ (accessed on 1 December 2018).
61 COM(2016) 385 final.
62 http://www.consilium.europa.eu/media/21645/28-euco-conclusions.pdf (accessed on 30 November 2018).
63 COM(2016) 385 final, p. 3.
64 Ibidem.

migration",[65] with a combination of short- and long-term objectives. The declared short-term goals are to save lives at sea, enhance returns of irregular migrants and "enable migrants and refugees to stay close to home".[66] To this end, immediate action should be taken with key partners to improve the legislative framework on migration and offer concrete assistance for capacity building on border and migration management, including protection for refugees "to stem the irregular flows while offering legal migration channels".[67] In the long run, the EU should continue to increase its efforts to address the political, social, economic and environmental factors that constitute the root causes of migration. As enounced,

> the ultimate aim of the Partnership Framework is a coherent and tailored engagement where the Union and its Member States act in a coordinated manner putting together instruments, tools and leverage to reach comprehensive partnerships *(compacts)* with third countries to better manage migration in full respect of our humanitarian and human rights obligations.[68]

However, despite the explicit references to refugees protection and human rights obligations,[69] the emphasis is on stemming irregular migration through the return of migrants, having recourse to 'all

---

65 Bauloz, Cèline, "The EU Migration Partnership Framework: an External Solution to the Crisis?", in *EU Immigration and Asylum Law and Policy*, 31 January 2017, available at http://eumigrationlawblog.eu/the-eu-migration-partnership-framework-an-external-solution-to-the-crisis/ (accessed on 7 October 2018).

66 COM(2016) 385 final, p. 6.

67 Ibidem.

68 The idea of 'migration compacts' has been first suggested by the former Italian Prime Minister, Matteo Renzi, on 15 April 2016: see http://www.governo.it/sites/governo.it/files/immigrazione_0.pdf. Afterwards, it has been envisaged also in the New York Declaration for Refugees and Migrants of September 2016, available at http://www.un.org/ga/search/view_doc.asp?symbol=A/71/L.1 (accessed on 30 November 2018). For a comparison between the EU policy and the New York Declaration, see Almeida, Gabriel, Bamberg, Katharina, "The UN Summit for Refugees and Migrants: A Mirror of the Current EU Migration Policy?" in *EU Immigration and Asylum Law and Policy*, 24 November 2017, available at http://eumigrationlawblog.eu/the-un-summit-for-refugees/ (accessed on 30 November 2018) and more recently, Vitiello, Daniela, "Il contributo dell'Unione europea alla governance internazionale dei flussi di massa di rifugiati e migranti: spunti per una rilettura critica dei Global Compacts", in *Diritto, Immigrazione e Cittadinanza*, N. 3, 2018, p. 1 ff., available at https://www.dirittoimmigrazionecittadinanza.it/saggi/304-saggio-vitiello/file (accessed on 3 November 2018) and literature quoted therein.

69 COM(2016) 385 final, in particular p. 6.

means available',[70] which implies, as specified in the Communication, "a mix of positive and negative incentives and the use of *all leverages and tools*".[71] This is particularly worrisome considering the countries of origin and transit selected with which to launch compacts: Mali, Nigeria, Niger, Senegal and Ethiopia.[72]

Moreover, the Communication establishes a strict relationship between aid to development and cooperation on migration management. Indeed, the Communication affirms:

> The compacts will be the key components of the overall relationships between the EU and third countries of origin or transit of migrants. These relationships will be guided by the ability and willingness of the countries to cooperate on migration management, notably in effectively preventing irregular migration and readmitting irregular migrants...[73]
>
> Positive and negative incentives should be integrated in the EU's development policy, rewarding those countries that fulfil their international obligation to readmit their own nationals, and those that cooperate in managing the flows of irregular migrants from third countries....[74]

As pointed out, by doing so, the MPF is not pursuing the 2030 Agenda for Sustainable Development goals, undertaken by all Member States through, *inter alia*, the facilitation of orderly, safe, regular and responsible migration and mobility of people (target 10.7), but on the contrary, "uses sustainable development as a leverage for stemming migration".[75]

Those two shortfalls – the lack of proportionality between the aim of reducing flows of irregular migrants and protection of migrants' rights on the one hand, and the conditionality of aid development to cooperation in migration containment on the other – are even more evident in the following Summit Conclusions and Communications, with a disturbing novelty: the progressive indication of Libya as a key pawn.

The European Council Conclusions of 28 June 2016 already contained a clear endorsement of "the expanded role for Operation Sophia

70 Ibidem, p. 2.
71 Ibidem, p. 6.
72 Ibidem, p. 19.
73 COM(2016) 385 final p. 6.
74 COM(2016) 385 final, p. 9.
75 See Bauloz, cit.

in ... training the Libyan Coast Guard".[76] Therefore the mandate of European Union Naval Force Mediterranean (EUNAVFOR MED, also called Operation Sophia) – an EU military operation established on 18 May 2015 to contribute "to the disruption of the business model of human smuggling and trafficking networks in the South Central Mediterranean"[77] – was modified to embrace capacity building and training of the Libyan Coast Guard.[78]

In even more unambiguous words, the European Commission, in its Joint Communication of 25 January 2017,[79] declares that:

> To effectively cope with this current situation, part of the answer must lie in the Libyan authorities preventing smugglers from operating, and for the Libyan Coast Guard to have the capacity to better manage maritime border and ensure safe disembarkation on the Libyan coast. Of course, the Libyan authorities' effort must be supported by the EU and Member States notably through training, providing advice, capacity building and other means of support.[80]

To this end, the Commission recommends making use of the entire range of EU missions[81] and projects to support the Libyan authorities.

Then, at the informal Summit held at La Valletta on 3 February 2017 (the day after the signing of the Italy-Libya MoU), the European

76 European Council, *Conclusions*, European Council meeting (28 June 2016), available at: www.consilium.europa.eu/press-releasespdf/2016/6/4724 4643506_en.pdf (10 /17), para. 19 (accessed on 30 November).

77 Decision (CFSP) 2015/778, Article 1. See *inter alia* Gestri, Marco, "Eunavfor Med: Fighting Migrant Smuggling Under UN Security Council Resolution 2240 (2015)", in *Italian Yearbook of International Law*, Vol. 25, 2016, p. 21 ff. and literature quoted therein.

78 https://publications.europa.eu/en/publication-detail/-/publication/112fece2-7719-11e6-b076-01aa75ed71a1 (accessed on 30 November).

79 European Commission, *Migration on the Central Mediterranean route Managing flows, saving lives*, Joint Communication to the European Parliament, the European Council and the Council of 25 January 2017, JOIN(2017) 4 final.

80 Ibidem, p. 6

81 Therefore, the mandate of the EU Border Assistance Mission in Libya (EUBAM), a civilian Mission established on 22 May 2013 under the Common Security and Defence Policy (CSDP), was extended to "advice and capacity-building in the area of...migration [and] border security": see EUBAM Libya: mission extended, budget approved, EC Press Release, 4 Aug. 2016, available at http://www.consilium.europa.eu/en/press/press-releases/2016/08/04-eubam-libya-mission-extended/ (accessed on 16 November 2018).

Council agrees to a Declaration (known as the *Malta Declaration*) concerning the Central-Mediterranean route,[82] which states *inter alia* that:

> "Where possible the EU and Member States will also step up cooperation with and assistance to Libyan regional and local communities and with international organizations active in the country" and that "Priority will be given to … training, equipment and support to the Libyan national coast guard and other relevant agencies".[83]

Consequently, in its Action Plan of 4 July 2017, the Commission decides to further enhance the capacity of the Libyan authorities through a €46 million project (developed jointly with Italy) and to support the establishment of a fully operational Maritime Rescue and Coordination Centre in Libya.

The increasing accusations in several reports of non-governmental and governmental organizations, testifying about torture and inhuman treatment of migrants in detention camps in Libya,[84] as well as a BBC video on the slave market of migrants in Libya,[85] led finally to the creation of a Task Force on migration. On 28 November 2017, the United Nations Secretary-General, Antonio Guterres, the Chairperson of the African Union Commission, Moussa Faki Mahamat, the President of the European Commission, Jean-Claude Juncker and the High Representative/Vice President, Federica Mogherini, met on the margins of the African Union/European Union Summit in Abidjan and

> agreed to put in place a joint EU-AU-UN Task Force to save and protect lives of migrants and refugees along the routes and

---

82 European Council, *Declaration concerning the Central-Mediterranean route* (Malta Declaration), adopted on 3 February 2017, available at: www.consilium.europa.eu/en/press/press-releases/2017/01/03-malta-declarati on/ (accessed on 16 November 2018).

83 Because of its political and financial support, the EU has also been accused of complicity for the serious violations committed in Libya vis-à-vis migrants (see Amnesty International report *Libya's Dark Web of Collusion*, available at https://www.amnesty.org/en/documents/mde19/7561/2017/en/, p. 60) (accessed on 30 November 2018). An analysis on the responsibility of the European Union is outside the scope of this work.

84 See supra Part I, § 2.

85 See BBC video of October 2017 available at https://edition.cnn.com/specials/africa/libya-slave-auctions (accessed on 16 November 2018).

in particular inside Libya, accelerating the assisted voluntary returns to countries of origin, and the resettlement of those in need of international protection,[86]

with the cooperation of the International Organization for Migration (IOM) and UNHCR. To this end, UNHCR established the Emergency Evacuation Transit Mechanism (ETM), providing evacuation to Niger for the most vulnerable refugees detained in Libya, while seeking more durable solutions (i.e. resettlement).

This initiative, which is positive in intent, is however completely insufficient. First of all, it does not address the major shortfalls of the current situation, i.e. EU financing Libya notwithstanding the latter still detains migrants in inhuman conditions. Second, the number of people who should profit from it is limited (a few thousand) if we compare it to the hundreds of thousands still trapped in Libya in unofficial detention centres, where neither the UNHCR nor NGOs can have access. This second argument is even stronger if we look at the numbers of those actually affected by the above-mentioned mechanism: so far only around 2,000 people have been evacuated from Libya to Niger[87] and only a few hundred have actually been resettled to Europe.[88]

At the EU Summit of 28 June 2018, externalization received new inputs for a number of reasons: the unsatisfactory situation caused by the Dublin regulation, born in a different historical context but completely inadequate to face the current challenges, since it imposes the major burden of asylum determination only on the countries of first arrival (Greece and Italy above all, but recently also Spain); the refusal of the countries belonging to the Visegrad group (the Czech Republic, Hungary, Poland and Slovakia) to do their part in the relocation process, conversely adopting praxis and legislations more and more in violation of migrants' rights[89]; the irresponsible attitude of Italy,

---

86 http://europa.eu/rapid/press-release_STATEMENT-17-5029_en.htm (accessed on 30 November).

87 https://reliefweb.int/report/libya/unhcr-flash-update-libya-2-9-nov-2018-enar (accessed on 30 November).

88 http://reporting.unhcr.org/sites/default/files/UNHCR%20Libya-Niger%20 Situation%20Resettlement%20Update%20-%2013MAY18.pdf (accessed on 30 November).

89 The case of Hungary is emblematic: see Nagy, Boldizsár, "Renegade in the Club – Hungary's Resistance to EU Efforts in the Asylum Field", in *Osteuropa-RECHT*, 2017, p. 413 ff., available at https://www.researchgate.net/publication/323447046_ Renegade_in_the_Club_-_Hungary's_Resistance_to_EU_Efforts_in_the_Asylum_ Field (accessed on 5 December 2018).

characterized by an increasingly hostile attitude vis-à-vis NGOs engaged in rescue operations in the Central Mediterranean Sea, which reached its peak in June 2018, when a populist coalition came to power, forbidding NGOs, commercial and even boats belonging to the Italian Coast Guard from docking in Italian harbours.[90] All this led to the very dismal conclusions of the EU Summit of 28–29 June 2018. With regard to Libya, European leaders explicitly provided for further support to the Libyan Coast Guard and ordered "all vessels operating in the Mediterranean ... not to obstruct operation of the Libyan Coast Guard". A sinister pre-endorsement of what would happen in the same hours in the Mediterranean: on 29 June 2018, the NGO boat Astral was prevented from rescuing a boat, although it was already *sur place*, because the Italian IMRCC had ordered that the Libyan coastguard was to respond to the distress call. This however had a dramatic ending, because immediately afterwards "100 migrants were missing and feared dead in the same area".[91]

In the same summit, the European Council called on the Council and the Commission "to swiftly explore the concept of regional disembarkation platforms, in close cooperation with relevant third countries as well as UNHCR and IOM",[92] adding that "Such platforms should operate distinguishing individual situations, in full respect of international law and without creating a pull factor". This proposal had already been the object of analysis by UNHCR and IOM (*Proposal for a regional cooperative arrangement ensuring predictable disembarkation and subsequent processing of persons rescued-at-sea*),[93] sent on

---

90 See *supra*, Part. 1, § 5.
91 https://www.theguardian.com/world/2018/jun/29/italy-and-libya-accused-after-migrant-deaths-in-dinghy-sinking (accessed on 30 November).
92 See Collett, Elizabeth, Fratzke, Susan, "Europe Pushes to Outsource Asylum, Again", *Migration Policy Institute*, June 2018, available at https://www.migration-policy.org/news/europe-pushes-outsource-asylum-again/ (accessed on 7 October 2018); Di Filippo, Marcello, "Unione europea e flussi migratori, o del tramonto dello spirito comunitario: considerazioni a margine del Consiglio europeo del 28-29 giugno 2018", *SIDIBlog*, 9 July 2018, available at http://www.sidiblog.org/author/marcello-di-filippo/ (accessed on 7 October 2018); Maiani, Francesco, "'Regional Disembarkation Platforms' and 'Controlled Centres': Lifting The Drawbridge, Reaching out Across The Mediterranean, or Going Nowhere?", in *EU Immigration and Asylum Law and Policy*, 18 September 2018, available at http://eumigration lawblog.eu/regional-disembarkation-platforms-and-controlled-centres-lifting-the-drawbridge-reaching-out-across-the-mediterranean-or-going-nowhere/ (accessed on 7 October 2018).
93 http://www.unhcr.org/partners/eu/5b35e60f4/proposal-regional-cooperative-arrangement-ensuring-predictable-disembarkation.html (accessed on 30 November).

27 June 2018 to the President of the European Council, Donald Tusk. On 24 July 2018, the European Commission adopted a *Non-paper on regional disembarkation arrangements*, based on the joint UNHCR and IOM above-mentioned proposal.[94]

The idea of establishing offshore centres for the processing of asylum requests is not new in the European debate and had already been criticized by scholars both from a practical and juridical point of view.[95] Indeed, after having been refused by most potentially interested African countries,[96] it is not clear whether, where or when such disembarkation platforms will be established: on 26 October 2018, the European Commission President, Jean-Claude Juncker declared that North Africa camps were no longer on the EU agenda,[97] while at the end of November 2018, the *EU Observer*[98] reported that according to Vincent Piket, a senior official in the EU's foreign policy branch, the EEAS, "the discussion is proceeding in the Council" and that the Legal Service of the European Parliament has prepared a confidential report stating *inter alia* that disembarkation platforms could lawfully

94 https://ec.europa.eu/home-affairs/sites/homeaffairs/files/what-we-do/policies/european-agenda-migration/20180724_non-paper-regional-disembarkation-arrangements_en.pdf (accessed on 30 November).

95 See *ex multis* Noll, Gregor, "Visions of the Exceptional: Legal and Theoretical Issues Raised by Transit Processing Centres and Protection Zones", in *European Journal of Migration and Law*, Vol. 5, N. 3, 2003, pp. 338 ff.; Francis, Angus, "Bringing Protection Home: Healing the Schism Between International Obligations and National Safeguards Created by Extraterritorial Processing", in *International Journal of Refugee Law*, Vol. 20, N. 2, 2008, p. 273 ff. and more recently, Liguori, Anna, "Some Observations on the Legal Responsibility", cit.; Guild, Espelth, Carrera, Sergio, Offshore Processing of Asylum Applications: Out of Sight, Out of Mind?, in *CEPS Commentary*, 27 January 2017, available at https://www.ceps.eu/publications/offshore-processing-asylum-applications-out-sight-out-mind (accessed on 7 October 2018); Carrera, Sergio et al., "Offshoring Asylum and Migration in Australia, Spain, Tunisia and the US: Lessons Learned and Feasibility for the EU", in *CEPS Commentary*, 18 September 2018, available at https://www.ceps.eu/publications/offshoring-asylum-and-migration-australia-spain-tunisia-and-us (accessed on 7 October 2018).

96 https://www.politico.eu/article/eu-cant-outsource-migration-crisis-disembarkation-platforms-centers/ (accessed on 7 October 2018).

97 https://www.reuters.com/article/us-europe-migrants-africa/juncker-says-north-africa-migrant-camps-not-on-eu-agenda-idUSKCN1N01TU (accessed on 30 November). Austria and Italy in September proposed a plan to process refugees on ships https://www.dw.com/en/austria-italy-propose-processing-refugees-on-ships/a-45496615, but also this idea has not yet been followed-up.

98 https://euobserver.com/migration/143513 (accessed on 28 November 2018).

be established outside of the European Union, in order to receive migrants rescued outside the territory of the Union's member states".

Indeed, in the conclusions of the European Council of 18 October 2018,[99] the idea of establishing regional disembarkation centres was ignored,[100] while "a list of non-specific conclusions was agreed to",[101] including "cooperation with countries of origin and transit, particularly in North Africa, as part of a broader partnership" and "work with third countries on investigating, apprehending and prosecuting smugglers and traffickers … with a view to preventing people from embarking on perilous journeys". To this end, the Council, with the support of the Commission, is explicitly invited to propose an operational set of measures by December 2018.[102]

99 https://www.consilium.europa.eu/media/36775/18-euco-final-conclusions-en.pdf (accessed on 30 November).
100 Also the idea – envisaged in the EU Council conclusions of 28 June 2018 – of extending the mandate of the European Border and Coast Guard Agency is not mentioned in these conclusions. On this idea, see however the critical position of Maccaninco, Yasha, "Morocco: Wherever EU Immigration Policy ears its ugly head, violence and abuses follow", available at http://www.statewatch.org/analyses/no-334-morocco-migration-expulsions.pdf, accessed on 30 October 2018, who esteems that such a reform might turn it "into a fully-fledged border guard with executive powers to institutionalize the dogged harassment of migrants".
101 See Frenzen, Niels, "European Council Conclusions on Migration, 18 October 2018", in *Migrants At Sea Blog*, of 19 October 2018, available at https://migrantsat-sea.org/2018/10/19/european-council-conclusions-on-migration-18-october-2018/ (accessed on 30 November 2018).
102 Ibidem.

2 The attitude of the Luxembourg Court vis-à-vis externalization

While examining EU policies on extraterritorial border controls, it is worth taking a quick overview of the recent decisions of the European Court of Justice vis-à-vis two aspects of EU externalization – i.e. the EU-Turkey orders (the General Court orders of 28 February 2017 and the European Court of Justice order of 12 September 2018 on appeal) and the Humanitarian Visa Judgment of 7 March 2017, in order to verify the actual role of the Luxembourg Court in ensuring that human rights – solemnly affirmed in the Treaty on the European Union both in general (Articles 2 and 6 TEU) and with specific regard to EU external action (Article 21 TEU) – are respected in such sensitive matters.

2.1 The case law concerning the EU-Turkey Statement

In three orders of 28 February 2017 – *NF, NG and NM v. European Council*[1] – the General Court dismissed the actions for annulment of the EU-Turkey statement – lodged by an Afghan national and two Pakistani nationals – as inadmissible. Since the General Court's approach and reasoning is the same in all three cases, to simplify matters we will only refer to the *NF v. European Council* case.

The applicant, a Pakistani asylum seeker risking to be sent back to Turkey, submitted an application for annulment under Article 263 Treaty on the Functioning of the European Union (TFEU) of the EU-Turkey agreement, alleging both human rights violations (incompatibility with EU fundamental rights, particularly Articles 1, 18 and 19 of the Charter of Fundamental Rights of the European Union) and constitutional issues (failure to comply with Article 218 TFEU).

The court limits its analysis to the question of whether it has jurisdiction, more specifically as to whether the statement is to be attributed to the EU, concluding, by an intricate reasoning, that this is not the case.

---

1 Orders of the General Court of 28 February 2017 cases T-192/16, T-193/16, T-257/16.

The Court starts by remembering that

> generally the European Union Courts have no jurisdiction to rule
> on the lawfulness of a measure adopted by a national authority
> (judgments of 3 December 1992, Oleificio Borelli v Commission,
> C-97/91, para. 9)…or measures adopted by the representatives of
> the Member States physically gathered in the grounds of one of
> the European Union institutions and acting, not in their capac-
> ity as members of the Council or European Council, but in their
> capacity as Heads of State or Government of the Member States
> of the European Union (judgment of 30 June 1993, Parliament v
> Council and Commission, C-181/91 and C-248/91, para. 12).[2]

It adds however, that

> In order to qualify a measure as a 'decision of the Member States'
> of the European Union,… it is still necessary to determine whether,
> having regard to its content and all the circumstances in which it
> was adopted, the measure in question is not in reality a decision
> of the European Council (judgment of 30 June 1993, *Parliament* v
> *Council and Commission*,C-181/91 and C-248/91, para. 14).[3]

The Court then stresses that the meeting of 18 March 2016 was the
third of three since November 2015, and that in the two previous meet-
ings (respectively, on 29 November 2015 and on 7 March 2016) it was
the representatives of the Member States who participated in their
capacity as Heads of State or Government of the Member States of
the European Union and not as Members of the European Council.
Afterwards, the Court admits that the wording of the statement, as
published following the meeting of 18 March 2016 by means of Press
Release No 144/16, was different from previous statements. However,
it adds that this is due "to simplification of the words used for the general public in the context of a press release" and expresses regret for
the ambiguity.

Finally, the Court goes on to explore a number of preparatory documents of the meeting of 18 March 2018, concluding that

> In those circumstances… the expression 'Members of the European
> Council' and the term 'EU', contained in the EU-Turkey state-
> ment as published by means of Press Release No 144/16, must be

---

2 Para. 44.
3 Para. 45.

understood as references to the Heads of State or Government of the European Union.[4]

The order has been criticized for many reasons.[5] First of all, it appears evident that relying on the wording of the Statement, which employs explicit terms ('Members of the European Council' and 'EU') "would have been more straightforward, and therefore more convincing than the one adopted by the court".[6] Indeed, the General Court most probably deliberately avoided such interpretation in order to avoid a difficult alternative. If it had examined the compatibility of the EU-Turkey Statement with European and international asylum and refugee law, it would either have come to a conclusion of nonconformity or have opted for a narrow interpretation of asylum and refugee law.[7] Both choices could have fuelled – for opposite reasons – a hot political situation.

In other words, the impression is that the Court exercised a sort of self-restraint to avoid taking a position on a sensitive issue. This attitude has also been qualified as "judicial passivism" (i.e. "the Court is consciously not using its powers where it should, thereby sending a message to the EU institutions and Member States"),[8] or as 'realism'.[9]

---

4 Para. 69.
5 Limone, Luigi, "Today's Court (Non) Decision on the (Non) EU "deal"? with Turkey", in *European Area of Freedom Security & Justice FREE Group*, 1 March 2017, available at https://free-group.eu/2017/03/01/the-todays-court-non-decision-on-the-non-eu-deal-with-turkey/, (accessed on 7 October 2018); Cannizzaro, "Denialism", cit.; Carrera, Sergio, Den Hertog, Leonhard, Stefan, Marco, "It Wasn't Me! The Luxembourg Court Orders on the EU-Turkey Refugee Deal", in *CEPS Policy Insights* N. 2017, 15, April 2017, available at https://www.ceps.eu/system/files/EU-Turkey%20Deal.pdf (accessed on 7 October 2018); Danisi, Carmelo, "Taking the 'Union' out of the 'EU': The EU-Turkey Statement on the Syrian Refugee Crisis as an Agreement Between States under International Law", in *European Journal of Int. Law: Talk!*, 20 April 2017, available at https://www.ejiltalk.org/taking-the-union-out-of-eu-the-eu-turkey-statement-on-the-syrian-refugee-crisis-as-an-agreement-between-states-under-international-law/ (accessed on 7 October 2018); Idriz, Narin, "Taking the EU-Turkey Deal to Court?", in *Verfassungsblog*, 20 December 2017, available at https://verfassungsblog.de/taking-the-eu-turkey-deal-to-court/, (accessed on 28 March 2018).
6 Spijkerboer, Thomas, "Bifurcation of People, Bifurcation of Law: Externalization of Migration Policy before the EU Court of Justice", in Journal of Refugee Studies, Vol. 31, N. 2, 2018, p. 224.
7 Ibidem.
8 Goldner Lang, Iris, Speech at "The Odysseus Network's 3rd Annual Conference: Conflict and Competence Between Law and Politics in EU Migration and Asylum Policies", Final Plenary Session, "Towards 'Judicial Passivism' in EU Migration and Asylum Law?", 1 February 2018, https://www.youtube.com/watch?v=x8U98 izwkyA (accessed on 30 November).
9 Cannizzaro, "Denialism", cit., p. 257.

Member States seem to forget when they think there is a 'crisis' that the EU is a legal order based on the rule of law and conferred powers.[10] The CJEU missed a good opportunity to authoritatively reaffirm this principle and conversely, set a dangerous precedent.

First of all, the Order contravenes the ERTA doctrine,[11] codified by the Lisbon Treaty in Article 3(2) TFEU, which states *inter alia* that "the Union shall also have exclusive competence for the conclusion of an international agreement in so far as its conclusion may affect common rules or alter their scope". As pointed out,[12]

> the Heads of State and Government of the MS do not have an unfettered power to select the capacity in which they are acting. By virtue of EU constitutional constraints, when the effect of their acts encroaches upon existing EU legislation, they lose their power to act outside the EU framework, as mere representatives of their States.

Therefore, the Court should not have investigated the 'intent' of persons wearing different hats at the same meeting, i.e. acting at times as representative of Member States, other times as part of the European Council and thus as EU. Conversely, it should have analyzed the content and all the circumstances in which the statement was adopted.[13] Indeed, as convincingly argued,[14]

> [t]he application of this test in the case at hand inexorably leads to the conclusion that an international instrument that plainly falls within the competence of the EU, negotiated by the President of the European Council and by the President of the European Commission – two organs entrusted with the international representation

10 Idriz, cit.
11 Court of justice, judgment of 31 March 1971, case 22/70, *Commission of the European Communities v. Council of the European Communities*, concerning the European Road Transport Agreement (ERTA).
12 Cannizzaro, "Denialism", cit., 253.
13 See CJEU, judgment of 30 June 1993, *European Parliament v. Council of the European Communities and Commission of the European Communities*, joined cases C-181/91 and C-248/91, para. 14.
14 See Cannizzaro, "Denialism", p. 256. Indeed, as above mentioned, an EU-Turkey Readmission Agreement had already been signed in 2013 and had entered into force on 1 October 2014, except its provisions relating to the readmission of third country nationals: these provisions were destined to enter into effect three years after the date of entry into force of the EU-Turkey Readmission Agreement: see Article 24(3).

of the EU –, adopted at a meeting of the European Council and Turkey held in the headquarters of the European Council, communicated in the form of a press release of the European Council and posted on its website, whose wording immediately conveys the idea that its consent has been agreed upon by Turkey and the EU, cannot but be attributed to the EU.

Moreover, choosing to place the EU-Turkey statement outside the scope of EU law is extremely regrettable also because by doing so the Court supports (instead of opposing) the approach of Member States and of EU institutions aiming at circumventing political and judicial controls (respectively by the European Parliament and the Court of Justice) by resorting to arrangements which do not fall within the scope of Article 218 TFUE. As pointed out,[15] "This case illustrates how the checks and balances built into the system can be completely bypassed when the EU institutions collude with Member States to act outside the Treaty framework".

The order was appealed, but unfortunately the Court dismissed it without examining it on the merits.[16] In fact, the Court observed that

> The appeals thus simply make general assertions that the General Court disregarded a certain number of principles of EU law, without indicating with the requisite degree of precision the contested elements in the orders under appeal or the legal arguments specifically advanced in support of the application for annulment.[17]

Referring to its previous case law,[18] the Court concludes that

> an appeal with such characteristics cannot be the subject of a legal assessment which would allow the Court of Justice to exercise its function in the area under examination and to carry out its review of legality,[19]

---

15 Idriz, cit. However, as pointed out (Rijpma, "External Migration and Asylum Management", cit., p. 25), "in its implementation the Member States must still be considered as acting within the scope of EU law when declaring an asylum request inadmissible or issuing a return decision".

16 CJEU, order of 12 September 2018, *NF, NG and NM v. European Council*, cases C-208/17 P, C-209/17 P and C-210/17 P.

17 Para. 16.

18 CJEU, judgment of 14 December 2016, *SV Capital* v *EBA*, case C-577/15 P, para. 69 and the case law quoted therein.

19 Para. 17.

adding that

> by their arguments, the appellants merely express their disagreement with the General Court's assessment of the facts, while requesting that those facts be assessed again, without claiming or establishing that the General Court's assessment of the facts is manifestly inaccurate, which is inadmissible in an appeal.[20]

As the documents for the appeal have yet to be published, a detailed comment on the approach taken by the Court is difficult: however, the impression is that the Court resorted to an "usage stratégique du droit procédural"[21] to avoid taking a stand in a controversial debate. Unfortunately, by doing so, it risks abdicating its role as guardian of the rule of law and sidestepping fundamental values which are the very foundations of the European Union.

2.2 The humanitarian visa judgment of 7 March 2017

On 7 March 2017, the Court of Justice adopted another judgment considered expression of 'passivism'[22] in the case *X and X*.[23]

---

20 Para. 29.
21 See Van Malleghem, Pieter-Augustijn, "C.J.U.E., Aff. jointes C-208/17 P à C-210/17 P, ordonnance du 12 septembre 2018, NF, NG et NM, ECLI:EU:C:2018:705", in *Centre Charles De Visscher pour le droit international et européen*, 4 October 2018, available at https://uclouvain.be/fr/instituts-recherche/juri/cedie/actualites/c-j-u-e-aff-jointes-c-208-17-p-a-c-210-17-p-ordonnance-du-12-septembre-2018-nf-ng-et-nm.html#_ftn17 (accessed on 30 October 2018); see also Vitiello, "Il contributo dell'Unione europea", cit., p. 37.
22 Goldner Lang, Speech at "The Odysseus Network's 3rd Annual Conference", cit., 1 February 2018, available at https://www.youtube.com/watch?v=x8U98izwkyA (accessed on 30 October 2018).
23 CJEU, judgment of 7 March 2017, *X and X* [GC], case C-638/16 PPU. On this judgment, see Brouwer, Evelien, "The European Court of Justice on Humanitarian Visas: Legal integrity vs. political opportunism?", in *CEPS Commentary*, 16 March 2017, available at https://www.ceps.eu/system/files/Visa%20Code%20CJEU%20E%20 Brouwer%20CEPS%20Commentary_0.pdf, (accessed on 30 October 2018); De Vylder, Helena, "X and X v. Belgium: A Missed Opportunity for the CJEU to Rule on the State's Obligations to Issue Humanitarian Visa for Those in Need of Protection", in *Strasbourg Observer*, 14 April 2017, available at https://strasbourgobservers.com/2017/04/14/x-and-x-v-belgium-a-missed-opportunity-for-the-cjeu-to-rule-on-the-states-obligations-to-issue-humanitarian-visa-for-those-in-need-of-protection/, (accessed on 30 October 2018); Raimondo, Giulia, "Visti umanitari: il caso X e X contro Belgio, C-638/16 PPU", in *Sidiblog*, 1 May 2017, available at http://www.sidiblog.org/2017/05/01/visti-umanitari-il-caso-x-e-x-contro-belgio-c%E2%80%91163816-ppu/,

The case concerned a Syrian family who had come to Beirut (Lebanon) to apply at the Belgian Embassy for a territorially limited Schengen visa (LTV visa) on account of humanitarian considerations, in order to reach Belgium and request international protection there.[24] Judgment was delivered on the issue of preliminary ruling from the Conseil du Contentieux des Étrangers (Belgium) concerning the interpretation of Article 25(1)(a) of 'the Visa Code' and of Articles 4 and 18 of the Charter of Fundamental Rights of the European Union, asking in substance whether under the Visa Code Member States have the duty to issue a territorially limited Schengen visa, where there are substantial grounds to believe that the refusal to issue that document will have the direct consequence of exposing persons to torture or inhuman or degrading treatment.

In its judgment, the Court, although it acknowledged that the applicants in the main proceedings were facing a real risk of being subjected to inhuman and degrading treatment,[25] does not pronounce on the merits, but states that the application falls outside the scope of the Visa Code. This is because, in the Court's view, even if formally grounded on Article 25 of the Visa Code (concerning visas for intended stays of no more than three months), the application in reality was submitted "with a view to applying for asylum in Belgium immediately upon their arrival in that Member State and, thereafter, to being granted a residence permit with a period of validity not limited to 90 days".[26]

(accessed on 30 October 2018); Del Guercio, Adele, "La sentenza X. e X. della Corte di giustizia sul rilascio del visto umanitario:analisi critica di un'occasione persa", in *European Papers*, Vol.2, 2017, p. 271 ff. available at http://www.europeanpapers. eu/en/europeanforum/la-sentenza-x-e-x-della-corte-di-giustizia-sul-rilascio-del-visto-umanitario, (accessed on 30 October 2018); Favilli, Chiara, "Visti umanitari e protezione internazionale: così vicini così lontani", in *Diritti umani e Diritto internazionale*, N. 2, 2017, p. 553 ff., available at http://www.sidi-isil.org/wp-content/uploads/2017/04/Osservatorio-Favilli-per-SIDI.pdf (accessed on 30 October 2018); Cellamare, Giovanni, "Sul rilascio di visti di breve durata (VTL) per ragioni umanitarie", in *Studi sull'integrazione europea*, N. 3, 2017, p. 527 ff.; Calzavara, Felicita, "La *sentenza della Corte di giustizia in tema di visti umanitari: quando la stretta interpretazione rischia di svilire la dignità umana"*, in Ordine internazionale e diritti umani, 2017, p. 546 ff., available at http://www.rivistaoidu.net/sites/default/files/5_Calzavara_0.pdf, (accessed on 30 October 2018).

24 A similar case is pending before the European Court of Human Rights (ECtHR): see M. N. *and others v. Belgium*, applic. No 3599/18, communicated to the government on 26 April 2018.

25 Para. 33.

26 Para. 42.

As a consequence, the Court inferred that the provisions of the Charter, in particular Articles 4 and 18 thereof, referred to in the questions of the Belgian court, do not apply,[27] thus concluding that:

> an application for a visa with limited territorial validity made on humanitarian grounds by a third-country national, on the basis of Article 25 of the code, to the representation of the Member State of destination that is within the territory of a third country, with a view to lodging, immediately upon his or her arrival in that Member State, an application for international protection and, thereafter, to staying in that Member State for more than 90 days in a 180-day period, does not fall within the scope of that code but, as European Union law currently stands, *solely within that of national law.*[28]

One of principal shortfalls of the decision is that it puts the applicants outside the scope of EU law on the basis of the real intention of their application, which was to reach Belgium in order to apply for asylum. However, as convincingly argued by the Advocate General Mengozzi[29] in its Opinion of 7 February 2017:

> The intention of the applicants in the main proceedings to apply for refugee status once they had entered Belgium cannot alter the nature or purpose of their applications. In particular, that intention cannot convert them into applications for long-stay visas or place those applications outside the scope of the Visa Code and of EU law, contrary to the submissions of several Member States at the hearing before the Court. Depending on the interpretation that the Court will be led to give of Article 25 of the Visa Code…, such an intention could at the very most constitute a ground for refusal of the applications of the applicants in the main proceedings, pursuant to the rules of that code, but certainly not a ground for not applying that code.[30]

---

27 Para. 45.
28 Italics added.
29 Opinion of Advocate General Mengozzi delivered on 7 February 2017, case C-638/16 PPU *X and X.*
30 On this point, see also Moreno-Lax, Violeta, "Asylum Visas as an Obligation under EU Law: Case PPU C-638/16 X, X v État belge" (Part. I-II), in *EU Immigration and Asylum Law and Policy*, 16 and 21 February 2017, available at http://eumigration lawblog.eu/asylum-visas-as-an-obligation-under-eu-law-case-ppu-c-63816-x-x-v-etat-belge/ (accessed on 30 October 2018): "This would be tantamount to accepting,

The Opinion of the Advocate General, a long and rich exposition – if we compare it with the brief reasoning of the Court – deserves attention under a number of aspects, and it seems worthwhile to review it, even if synthetically. It is true that the possibility of applying for humanitarian visa has not been codified yet at European level, despite proposals in this direction.[31] However the Opinion of the Advocate general shows that another interpretation, one that might have allowed a solution more in conformity with human rights,[32] was possible.

Indeed, after having illustrated that the intention of the applicants was irrelevant, the Advocate General adds that:

> by issuing or refusing to issue a visa with limited territorial validity on the basis of Article 25 of the Visa Code, the authorities of the Member States adopt a decision concerning a document authorising the crossing of the external borders of the Member States, which is subject to a *harmonised set of rules* and act, therefore, *in the framework of and pursuant to EU law*.[33]

---

for instance, that failed asylum seekers were *ab initio* excluded from the remit of the Qualification Directive and the Asylum Procedures Directive because ex post, upon determination of their claims, it has been concluded that they did not qualify for refugee status or subsidiary protection. The fact that an application for either a visa or for international protection under EU law is dismissed on the merits (or even at the admissibility stage) cannot be confounded with the determination of whether the rules of the relevant instruments (i.e. the CCV or the QD+APD) apply to and govern the examination of the claim".

31 The recent proposal of reform of the Visa Code (COM(2018) 252 final, of 14 March 2018) does not introduce, however, rules concerning the issue of humanitarian visas (see on this proposal Vavoula, Niovi, "Of Carrots and Sticks: A Punitive Shift in the Reform of the Visa Code", in *EU Immigration and Asylum Law and Policy*, 5 September 2018, available at http://eumigrationlawblog.eu/of-carrots-and-sticks-a-punitive-shift-in-the-reform-of-the-visa-code (accessed on 30 October 2018). The European Parliament is currently drafting a legislative own-initiative report under Rule 45 of the Rules of Procedure, to require the Commission to present a separate legislative act on Humanitarian Visas: see http://www.europarl.europa.eu/cmsdata/150782/eprs-study-humanitarian-visas.pdf (accessed on 30 November 2018).

32 In literature, the possibility to recognize a legal access route under Article 25 of the Visa Code has been extensively discussed: see Jensen, Ulla Iben, *Humanitarian Visas: Options or Obligations?*, Study for the LIBE Committee of the European Parliament, 2014, available at http://www.epgencms.europarl.europa.eu/cmsdata/upload/eb469bdf-0e31-40bb-8c75-8db410ab13fc/Session_2_-_Study_Humanitarian_visas.pdf, (accessed on 7 October 2018), p. 16; Peers, Steve, "Do Potential Asylum-Seekers Have the Right to a Schengen Visa?", in *EU Law Analysis*, 20 January 2014, available at http://eulawanalysis.blogspot.com/2014/01/do-potential-asylum-seekers-have-right.html (accessed on 30 October 2018); Moreno-Lax, "Asylum Visas", cit.

33 Para. 80. Italics is in the Opinion.

He goes on to say that such a conclusion cannot be called in question by the circumstance that the Member State enjoyed discretion in applying Article 25(1)(a) of the Visa Code, because the Court of Justice has stated in a number of cases that acts adopted in the exercise of discretion fall within the scope of EU law.[34] He then concludes that by adopting a decision under Article 25 of the Visa Code, Member States implemented EU law and therefore were required to respect the rights guaranteed by the Charter.

He then goes on to analyze the merits of whether the discretion of the Member State had been exercised in conformity with the Charter. To this end, first of all, he recalls that in the judgment of 21 December 2011, *N. S. and Others*,[35] concerning the determination of the Member State responsible for processing an application for asylum, the Court stated that "a mere option for a Member State ... may turn into an actual obligation on that Member State in order to ensure compliance with Article 4 of the Charter".[36] He also stresses that this right corresponds to the right guaranteed by Article 3 of the European Convention on Human Rights (ECHR), and affirms that

> By analogy with the case-law of the European Court of Human Rights on Article 3 of the ECHR, Article 4 of the Charter imposes on the Member States, when implementing EU law, not only a negative obligation with respect to individuals, that is to say that it prohibits the Member States from using torture and inhuman or degrading treatment, but also a *positive obligation*, that is to say that it requires them to take measures designed to ensure that those individuals are not subjected to torture and inhuman or degrading treatment, in particular in the case of vulnerable individuals, including where such ill-treatment is administered by private individuals.[37]
>
> ... In examining whether a State has failed to fulfil its positive obligation to adopt reasonable steps to avoid exposing a person to

---

34 See ex multis CJEU, *N. S. and Others*, cit., para. 68 and 69.
35 Cit., para. 94–98.
36 Para. 137.
37 Para. 139. Italics is in the text. To this end the Advocate General reminds that

> in its judgments of 21 December 2011, *N. S. and Others* ... (para. 106 and 113), and of 5 April 2016, *Aranyosi and Căldăraru* (C-404/15 and C-659/15 PPU, ... para. 90 and 94), the Court already held that, like Article 3 of the ECHR, Article 4 of the Charter imposes a positive obligation on the Member States under certain circumstances.

a genuine risk of treatment prohibited by Article 4 of the Charter, it is necessary, in my view, to ascertain, by analogy with the case-law of the European Court of Human Rights relating to Article 3 of the ECHR, what the foreseeable consequences of that omission or that refusal to act with regard to the person concerned are.[38]

Since the risks for the Syrian family were known or should have been known to the Belgian authorities, in light of the numerous reports attesting to the situation in Syria,[39] the Advocate General concludes that Article 25(1)(a) of the Visa Code must be interpreted as meaning that the Member State shall issue a LTV visa on humanitarian grounds if there are substantial grounds to believe that the refusal to issue that document will have the direct consequence of exposing that national to treatment prohibited by Article 4 of the Charter.[40]

The Opinion of the Advocate General is remarkable also with respect to the explicit statement that

> the fundamental rights recognized by the Charter, which any authority of the Member States must respect when acting within the framework of EU law, are guaranteed to the addressees of the acts adopted by such an authority *irrespective of any territorial criterion*.[41]

This position, already convincingly upheld in literature,[42] is very important because it denotes a broader scope of application of the EU Charter in comparison to the ECHR. While the dominant case law of the Strasbourg Court sets 'effective control' as a threshold for

---

38 Para. 140.
39 See para. 142–147.
40 Para. 163.
41 Para. 89.
42 See Moreno-Lax, Violeta, Costello, Cathryn, "The Extraterritorial Application of the EU Charter of Fundamental Rights: From Territoriality to Facticity, the Effectiveness Model", in *The EU Charter of Fundamental Rights: A Commentary* (S. Peers, T. Hervey, J. Kenner, A. Ward eds), Oxford, Hart Publishing, 2014, p. 1680: to this end, the authors quote the CJEU, judgment of 26 February 2013, *Åkerberg Fransson* [GC], case C-617/10, par. 21, which states that "[the applicability of European Union law entails applicability of the fundamental rights guaranteed by the Charter"; see also Moreno-Lax, *Accessing asylum in Europe*, cit., p. 472 and Rijpma, Jorrit, "External Migration and Asylum Management: Accountability for Executive Action Outside EU-territory", in *European Papers*, N. 2, 2017, p. 79, available at http://www.europeanpapers.eu/en/system/files/pdf_version/EP_eJ_2017_2_7_Article_Jorrit_J_Rijpma.pdf (accessed on 30 October 2018).

triggering jurisdiction under the ECHR (although, as noted above, there are cases which point to a different approach),[43] according to such interpretation, both EU institutions and the Member States, whenever they act within the scope of EU law, even outside the EU's borders, are bound by the Charter. In other words, the European Union has the duty to respect the rights guaranteed by the Charter "whenever it exercises its competences, both internally and externally, either directly or through the intermediation of the Member States 'implementing EU law'".[44]

Finally, it is worthwhile to compare the statement of the Luxembourg Court, affirming that "to conclude otherwise ... would undermine the general structure of the system established by Regulation No 604/2013"[45] (the Dublin regulation), and the premise enounced by the Advocate General at the beginning of his opinion, i.e. that "It is... crucial that, at a time when borders are closing and walls are being built, the Member States do not escape their responsibilities, as they follow from EU law".[46] In the first case, the Court is concerned with the consequences that would result from a · different interpretation of Article 25 of the Visa Code, because this would entail legal access irrespective of the rules established under the Dublin system; on the other hand, the Advocate General explicitly affirms that

> It is, on the contrary, the refusal to recognize a legal access route to the right to international protection on the territory of the Member States – which unfortunately often forces nationals of third countries seeking such protection to join, risking their lives in doing so, the current flow of illegal immigrants to EU's borders — which seems to me to be particularly worrying, in the light, inter alia, of the humanitarian values and respect for human rights on which European construction is founded.[47]

From this comparison, it is clear that the Court probably made a self-restraint because of the concern expressed by the 14 intervening Member States regarding an excessive augmentation of requests for

43 See *supra* Part I, § 4.2.1 and § 4.2.2.
44 Moreno-Lax, Costello, cit., p. 1682.
45 Judgment of 7 March 2017, cit., para. 48.
46 Opinion of Advocate General, Mengozzi, cit., para. 4.
47 Ibidem, para. 6.

visas at MS embassies in third countries.[48] The best answer to such fear, however, lies once again in Advocate General Mengozzi's words:

> Admittedly, the circle of persons concerned may prove to be wider than that which is currently the case in the practice of the Member States. That argument is however irrelevant in the light of the obligation to respect, in all circumstances, fundamental rights of an absolute nature, including the right enshrined in Article 4 of the Charter.[49]

48 See Del Guercio, cit., p. 285.
49 Ibidem, para. 171.

3 Closing remarks

This brief overview shows that externalization is on the top of the European Union agenda, despite the risks of serious violations of migrants' human rights. Libya is only the most blatant case, but serious concerns have also been raised with regard to the EU-Turkey statement, and in general to the increase of deals/pacts/memoranda with unsafe third countries without respecting the procedures established in the Treaty on the Functioning of the European Union (TFEU) for the conclusions of agreements, thus precluding a political (by the European Parliament) and judicial (by the Court of Justice) control.

This is particularly worrying in light of the formal commitment of the European Union to ensure respect of the rule of law and human rights.

Indeed, in the Treaty on the European Union (TEU), Article 2 emphatically states that

> The Union is founded on the values of respect for human dignity, freedom, democracy, equality, the rule of law and respect for human rights.

while Article 6 adds that:

> The Union recognizes the rights, freedoms and principles set out in the Charter of Fundamental Rights of the European Union of 7 December 2000, as adapted at Strasbourg, on 12 December 2007, which shall have the same legal value as the Treaties.

and that

> Fundamental rights, as guaranteed by the European Convention for the Protection of Human Rights and Fundamental Freedoms

and as they result from the constitutional traditions common to the Member States, shall constitute general principles of the Union's law

Such a solemn commitment is reiterated in Article 21 TEU with specific regard to the Union's External Action:

The Union's action on the international scene shall be guided by the principles which have inspired its own creation, development and enlargement, and which it seeks to advance in the wider world: democracy, the rule of law, the universality and indivisibility of human rights and fundamental freedoms, respect for human dignity, the principles of equality and solidarity, and respect for the principles of the United Nations Charter and international law.

Nevertheless, the CJEU, which in the past has shown a creative and progressive approach in dealing with national sovereign powers, also in migration matters,[1] seems to have abjured such a role when confronting delicate issues concerning externalization.

In fact, in the two cases analyzed above, the Court of Luxembourg has deliberately chosen, by recurring to hyper formalistic reasoning, a *modus interpretandi* which passes the buck to the States. Indeed, in the first case, in its controversial orders of 28 February 2017, the General Court denied its direct involvement in the so called EU-Turkey deal, saying that

it was in their capacity as Heads of State or Government of the Member States that the representatives of those Member States met with the Turkish Prime Minister on 18 March 2016 in the premises shared by the European Council and the Council.[2]

The order was challenged before the Court of Justice (CJEU), but the hope of a possible *revirement* was crushed subsequent to a new formalistic decision of inadmissibility of 12 September 2018, given the alleged 'unsubstantiated'[3] nature of the appeal.

Similarly, also in the judgment *X and X* of 7 March 2017 the Court of Justice adopted a self-restraint decision, stating that the granting of

---

1 See Costello, Cathryn, *The Human Rights of Migrants and Refugees in European Law*, Oxford, Oxford University Press, 2016.

2 Order of the General Court, 28 February 2017, cit., para. 66.

3 Order of the Court of Justice of 12 September 2018, cit., para. 24.

humanitarian visas does not fall within the scope of EU law but solely within that of national law, notwithstanding the fact that Advocate General Mengozzi had convincingly suggested a different possible interpretation.

What is particularly regretful is that a more courageous approach of the Court of Luxembourg might have offered a concrete possibility to affirm the supremacy of human rights also with regard to externalized border controls, given the extraterritorial applicability of the European Charter, as analyzed above.[4]

4 See *supra*, § 2.2.

Conclusions

The present work explores a current aspect of migration law, externalization of border controls, a widespread practice both on a European and non-European level, and which, regarding the former, refers both to the European Union as a whole and to the individual Member States. The point of view I have chosen is that of international responsibility: my specific intent being to explore whether outsourcing European States are responsible for human rights violations that arise as a consequence of such externalized migration controls and to determine the basis for their responsibility under international law. Even though my investigation does not provide definitive responses to all concerns arising in this complex area, it seeks to highlight some key issues, and at the same time, to propose a possible interpretation to some debated questions, such as the notion of jurisdiction under the European Convention on Human Rights (ECHR).

Before drawing any general conclusions, it seems of paramount importance to stress that European externalized migration controls might engage, directly or indirectly, multiple actors: Third States; EU Member States; the EU and/or EU agencies, such as the European Border and Coast Guard Agency (Frontex); CFSP (Common Foreign and Security Policy) missions (such as EUNAVFOR MED, European Union Naval Force Mediterranean); International Organizations such as the UNHCR (United Nations High Commissioner for Refugees) and IOM (International Organization for Migration); NGOs and/or private actors (for instance, private agencies for the issue of visas). The premise of this work is that in case of human rights violations as a consequence of externalization, there might be a shared responsibility[1]

---

1 By the expression "shared responsibility", we mean "responsibility of multiple actors for their contribution to a single harmful outcome". See Nollkaemper, André,

between the third State, the outsourcing State and/or the International Organizations involved, *in primis* the European Union. The question of whether the European Union might be held responsible and on what basis is indeed very important, in light of the support provided by, and frequently even the direct involvement of, the European Union in externalized migration controls. Furthermore, the European Union solemnly committed to respect human rights, in Articles 2 and 6 TEU in general and in Article 21 TEU with specific regard to EU external action. The question of EU responsibility therefore deserves an in-depth analysis, which is however outside the scope of this work, since my aim was rather to investigate State responsibility and in particular to explore the possibility of bringing a claim before the European Court of Human Rights (ECtHR).

Such an investigation is decidedly imperative in light of the recent attitude of the Luxembourg Court vis-à-vis two aspects of externalization of border controls (the EU-Turkey statement and the issue of humanitarian visas). The refusal to analyze the merits of both cases – on one hand, declining to be part of the so called EU-Turkey deal, and on the other, affirming that the issue fell outside the scope of European law – seems to pass the buck to Member States and thus confirms the importance of exploring the possibility of bringing claims before the Strasbourg Court.

This work draws on a topical example, the 2017 Italy-Libya Memorandum of Understanding – emblematic of the risk of human rights violations arising from externalization – claiming that, at least with respect to violation of the prohibition of torture, Italy should be held responsible for complicity.

Mutatis mutandis, complicity may apply also to other typologies of externalized migration controls. However, the exact meaning of the

Dov Jacobs, "Shared Responsibility in International Law: A Conceptual Framework", in *Michigan Journal of International Law*, Vol. 34, N. 2, 2013, p. 367. For an analysis of the thesis of a shared responsibility in case of offshore centres for processing asylum seekers, and in particular, with regard to the possibility of *dual attribution* of the same conduct both to a State and an IO, see Liguori, "Some observations on the legal responsibility", cit., p. 150 ff. and literature quoted therein. With specific regard to the possibility of "shared jurisdiction", in case of a plurality of States, see Gammeltoft-Hansen, Hathaway, cit., p. 272 ff. See also Den Heijer, Maarten, "Issues of Shared Responsibility before the European Court of Human Rights", Shares Research Paper N. 4, 2012, available at http://www.shares project.nl/wp-content/uploads/2012/01/Den-Heijer-Maarten-Issues-of-Shared-Responsibility-before-the-European-Court-of-Human-Rights-ACIL-2012-041.pdf (accessed on 7 October 2018).

requirements laid down in Article 16 ASR is debatable, especially with respect to 'the mental' element. This is why I explored an alternative basis for establishing responsibility. Indeed, as analyzed in detail in Part I, most of the objections which might be raised against complicity vis-à-vis European outsourcing States may be overcome if we explore responsibility on a different basis, i.e. as arising not from aid and assistance to the wrongful act but from the breach of positive obligations.

Resorting to the theory of positive obligations could in fact provide a useful alternative to the notion of complicity for a number of reasons. First, because when applying the theory of positive obligations, a court does not need to take into consideration the conduct of another State; second, because the requirement of 'knowledge' provided for by Article 16 of the ILC Articles on State Responsibility for complicity is more difficult to meet than the requisite that the State "know or ought to know", which is sufficient in the case of positive obligations; third, and most importantly, in the case under review, according to some elements of the jurisprudence of the ECtHR on positive obligations, analyzed in detail in Part I of this work, it might be easier to meet the jurisdiction requirement – which is the most difficult hurdle to overcome – thus facilitating the search for an effective remedy and holding outsourcing States accountable under the ECHR. Current externalized border controls assume different forms, from the provision of financial, technical, technological support to third countries to prevent departures, to typologies of cooperation entailing a stronger direct involvement by European States. As noted, "these new, cooperation-based *non-entrée* policies are rarely as 'hands off' as developed states like to suggest"[2] and thus a case by case analysis is essential. Because the concept of jurisdiction as "effective control" sets too high a threshold, however, it risks failing in most cases of externalized controls where the State does not enjoy direct control, but only exercises some kind of influence (such as signing border control agreements with third States: i.e. the case of the Italy-Libya MoU, under examination in this book). In all such situations, according to the circumstances of the case, the theory of positive obligations could be a useful tool to hold outsourcing States responsible, because in some cases, the Strasbourg Court has been ready to accept a lower threshold for jurisdiction, disentangled from 'effective control', in claims related to positive obligations.

---

2 See Gammeltoft-Hansen, Hathaway, cit., p. 243.

In other words, the interpretation of Strasbourg case law on positive obligations advocated in this work might be applied even in the most difficult cases, where there is no jurisdictional link under the traditional notion of "effective control". This interpretation, which belongs to the domain of *lex ferenda* rather than *lex lata*, could also be useful in evaluating the proposal of establishing third country disembarkation centres, recently envisaged in the conclusions of the European Council of 28–29 June 2018. Indeed, one of the most problematic aspects of offshore centres[3] is identifying, in cases of violations of migrants' human rights, a jurisdictional link between the individuals concerned and the outsourcing State.

With specific reference to the case study of this work, at the time of writing, a number of claims have been lodged before the ECtHR, concerning the consequences of the 2017 Italy-Libya Memorandum of Understanding.[4] Although the Strasbourg Court has solemnly affirmed on many occasions that States' sovereignty as regards immigration policy does not allow for recourse, in managing migratory flows, to practices that are not compatible with the Convention or the Protocols thereto,[5] it is difficult to predict how the ECtHR will deal with the pending claims concerning the externalization of migration controls. However, it is of paramount importance to find a possible remedy for all those situations in which the jurisdictional threshold of 'effective control' is difficult to reach, in order to find a way to hold outsourcing States responsible when, operating under the motto "Out of sight, out of mind", they tend to make refugees and migrants, as well as the violation of their rights, invisible.[6]

---

3 See Liguori, "Some observations on the legal responsibility", cit., p. 158.

4 *S.S. and Others v. Italy*, applic. No 21660/18 and *C.O. and A.J. v. Italy*, applic. No 40396/18, presented on 8 May 2018 and not yet communicated to the government, concerning the incident of 6 November 2017, mentioned *supra*, at § 5 of Part I. In June 2018, another claim was lodged before the Strasbourg Court by two young Gambian men, who had been pulled back to Libya and then repatriated to their country of origin – the news was reported by the Italian newspaper *La Repubblica*: see https://rep.repubblica.it/pwa/venerdi/2018/08/08/news/immigrati_respingimenti-203662488/ (accessed on 30 November 2018). At the time of writing, the claim has yet to be registered.

5 See, most recently, ECtHR judgment *N.D. and T. v. Spain*, cit., para. 101.

6 See Gammeltoft-Hansen, *Access to Asylum*, cit. p. 240 and Guild, Carrera, "Offshore processing", cit.

Bibliography

Almeida, Gabriel, Bamberg, Katharina, "The UN Summit for Refugees and Migrants: A Mirror of the Current EU Migration Policy?", in *EU Immigration and Asylum Law and Policy*, 24 November 2017, available at http://eumigration lawblog.eu/the-un-summit-for-refugees/ (accessed on 7 October 2018).

Amerasinghe, Chittharanjan F., "The Essence of the Structure of International Responsibility", in *International Responsibility Today: Essays in Memory of Oscar Schachter* (M. Ragazzi ed), Leiden, Martinus Nijhoff, 2005, p. 3 ff.

Annoni, Alessandra, "La responsabilità internazionale dello Stato per *sparizioni forzate*", in *Rivista di diritto internazionale*, Vol. 88, N. 3, 2005, p. 267 ff.

Aust, Helmut P., *Complicity and the Law of State Responsibility*, Cambridge, Cambridge University Press, 2011.

Baldaccini, Annalise, "The External Dimension of the EU's Asylum and Immigration Policies: Old Concerns and New Approaches", in *Whose Freedom, Security and Justice? EU Immigration and Asylum Law and Policy* (A. Baldaccini, E. Guild, H. Toner eds), Oxford, Oxford University Press, 2007, p. 277 ff.

Bar-Tuvia, Shani, "Australian and Israeli Agreements for the Permanent Transfer of Refugees: Stretching Further the (Il)legality and (Im)morality of Western Externalization Policies", in *International Journal of Refugee Law*, Vol XX, 2018, p. 1 ff.

Battjes, Hemme, "Territoriality and Asylum Law: The Use of Territorial Jurisdiction to Circumvent Legal Obligations and Human Rights Law Responses", in *Netherlands Yearbook of International Law*, Vol. 47, 2016, p. 263 ff.

Bauloz, Cèline, "The EU Migration Partnership Framework: An External Solution to the Crisis?", in *EU Immigration and Asylum Law and Policy*, 31 January 2017, available at http://eumigrationlawblog.eu/the-eu-migration-partnership-framework-an-external-solution-to-the-crisis/ (accessed on 7 October 2018).

Baumgärtel, Moritz, "High Risk, High Reward: Taking the Question of Italy's Involvement in Libyan 'Pullback' Policies to the European Court of

Human Rights", in *European Journal of International Law: Talk!*, 14 May 2018, available at https://www.ejiltalk.org/high-risk-high-reward-taking-the-question-of-italys-involvement-in-libyan-pullback-policies-to-the-european-court-of-human-rights/ (accessed on 5 December 2018).

Bernard, Ryan, "Extraterritorial Immigration Control: What Role for Legal Guarantees?", in *Extraterritorial Immigration Control: Legal Challenges* (B. Ryan, V. Mitsilegas eds), Vol. 21, Leiden, Brill-Martinus Nijhoff, 2010, p. 1 ff.

Bernard, Ryan, Mitsilegas, Valsamis (eds), *Extraterritorial Immigration Control: Legal Challenges*, Leiden, Brill-Martinus Nijhoff, 2010.

Biondi, Paolo, "Italy Strikes Back Again: A Push-back's Firsthand Account", in *Border Criminologies*, 15 December 2017, available at https://www.law.ox.ac.uk/research-subject-groups/centre-criminology/centreborder-criminologies/blog/2017/12/new-dutch (accessed on 7 October 2018).

Brouwer, Evelien, "The European Court of Justice on Humanitarian Visas: Legal integrity vs. Political Opportunism?", in *CEPS Commentary*, 16 March 2017, available at https://www.ceps.eu/system/files/Visa%20Code%20CJEU%20E%20Brouwer%20CEPS%20Commentary_0.pdf (accessed on 30 October 2018).

Brownlie, Ian, *System of the Law of Nations: State Responsibility Part 1*, Oxford, Oxford University Press, 1983.

Burlyuk, Olga, "The 'Oops!' of EU Engagement Abroad: Analyzing Unintended Consequences of EU External Action", in *Journal of Common Market Studies*, Vol. 55, N. 5, 2017, p. 1009 ff.

Caggiano, Giandonato, "Alla ricerca di un nuovo equilibrio istituzionale per la gestione degli esodi di massa: dinamiche intergovernative, condivisione delle responsabilità fra gli Stati membri e tutela dei diritti degli individui", in *Studi sull'integrazione europea*, Vol. X, 2015, p. 459 ff.

Caggiano, Giandonato, "Il processo decisionale dell'Unione europea a fronte del crescente sovranismo euroscettico. Ritorno al metodo intergovernativo per la "questione europea dell'immigrazione"?", in *Studi sull'integrazione europea*, 2018, p. 553 ff.

Calzavara, Felicita, "La *sentenza della Corte di giustizia in tema di visti umanitari: quando la stretta interpretazione rischia di svilire la dignità umana*" in *Ordine internazionale e diritti umani*, 2017, p. 546 ff., available at http://www.rivistaoidu.net/sites/default/files/5_Calzavara_0.pdf (accessed on 30 October 2018).

Cannizzaro, Enzo, "Disintegration Through Law?", in *European Papers*, 2016, p. 3 ff., available at Shttp://europeanpapers.eu/en/system/files/pdf_version/EP_eJ_2016_1_2_Editorial_EC.pdf (accessed on 7 October 2018).

Cannizzaro, Enzo, "Denialism as the Supreme Expression of Realism, A Quick Comment on NF v. European Council", in *European Papers*, 2017, p. 251 ff., available at http://www.europeanpapers.eu/it/system/files/pdf_version/EP_EF_2017_I_021_Enzo_Cannizzaro_4.pdf (accessed on 7 October 2018).

Carella, Gabriella, "Il sonno della ragione genera politiche migratorie", in *SIDIBlog*, 11 September 2017, available at http://www.sidiblog.org/2017/09/11/il-sonno-della-ragione-genera-politiche-migratorie/ (accessed on 7 October 2018).

Carlier, Jean-Yves, Crépeau, François, "Le droit européen des migrations: Exemple d'un droit en mouvement ?", in *Annuaire français de droit international*, Vol. 57, 2012, p. 641 ff.

Carrera, Sergio, Den Hertog, Leonhard, Stefan, Marco, "It Wasn't Me! The Luxembourg Court Orders on the EU-Turkey Refugee Deal", in *CEPS Policy Insights* N. 2017, 15, April 2017, available at https://www.ceps.eu/system/files/EU-Turkey%20Deal.pdf (accessed on 7 October 2018).

Carrera, Sergio et al., "Offshoring Asylum and Migration in Australia, Spain, Tunisia and the US: Lessons Learned and Feasibility for the EU", in *CEPS Commentary*, 18 September 2018, available at https://www.ceps.eu/publications/offshoring-asylum-and-migration-australia-spain-tunisia-and-us (accessed on 7 October 2018).

Casolari, Federico, "The EU's Hotspot Approach to Managing the Migration Crisis: A Blind Spot for International Responsibility?", in *The Italian Yearbook of International Law*, Vol. 25, 2016, p. 109 ff.

Casolari, Federico, "L'interazione tra accordi internazionali dell'Unione europea ed accordi conclusi dagli Stati membri con Stati terzi per il contrasto dell'immigrazione irregolare", in *Diritto, Immigrazione e Cittadinanza*, N. 1, 2018, pp. 1 ff.

Cassese, Antonio, "On the Use of Criminal Law Notions in Determining State Responsibility for Genocide", in *Journal of International Criminal Justice*, Vol. 5, 2007, p. 875 ff.

Cataldi, Giuseppe, "Giurisdizione e intervento in alto mare su navi impegnate nel traffico di migranti", in *Giurisprudenza italiana*, 2015, p. 1498 ff.

Cataldi, Giuseppe (ed), *A Mediterranean Perspective on Migrant Flows in The European Union: Protection of Rights, Intercultural Encounters and Integration Policies*, Napoli, Editoriale Scientifica, 2016.

Cataldi, Giuseppe, Liguori, Anna, Pace, Marianna (eds), *Migration in the Mediterranean Area and the Challenges for 'Hosting' European Societies*, Napoli, Editoriale Scientifica, 2017.

Cataldi, Giuseppe, "Migranti nel Mediterraneo e tutela dei diritti. Alcuni casi recenti della prassi italiana", in *Quaderni di economia sociale*, N. 2, 2018, p. 33 ff., available at https://www.sr-m.it/wp-content/uploads/woocommerce_uploads/2018/11/QES_2_18.pdf (accessed on 5 December 2018).

Cellamare, Giovanni, "In tema di «Paese sicuro» nel sistema europeo di asilo", in *Dialoghi con Ugo Villani* (E. Triggiani, F. Cherubini, I. Ingravallo, E. Nalin, R. Virzo eds), Tomo I, Bari, Cacucci Editore, 2017, p. 417 ff.

Cellamare, Giovanni, "Sul rilascio di visti di breve durata (VTL) per ragioni umanitarie", in *Studi sull'integrazione europea*, Vol. XII, N. 3, 2017, p. 527 ff.

Cellamare, Giovanni, "Note in margine alla sentenza della Corte europea dei diritti dell'uomo nell'affare N.D. e N.T. c. Spagna", in *Studi sull'integrazione europea*, Vol. XIII, N. 1, 2018, p. 153 ff.

Cerone, John, "Re-examining International Responsibility: "Complicity" in the Context of Human Rights Violations", in *ILSA Journal of International and Comparative Law*, Vol. 14, N. 2, 2008, p. 525–534, available at https://nsuworks.nova.edu/cgi/viewcontent.cgi?article=1625&context=ilsajournal/ (accessed on 7 October 2018).

Cherubini, Francesco (ed), *Le migrazioni in Europa. UE, Stati terzi e migration outsourcing*, Bordeaux, Roma, 2015.

Cherubini, Francesco, "The 'EU-Turkey Statement' of 18 March 2016: A (Umpteenth?) Celebration of Migration Outsourcing", in *Europe of Migrations: Policies, Legal Issues and Experiences* (S. Baldin, M. Zago eds), Trieste, EUT Edizioni Università di Trieste, 2017, p. 32 ff.

Chetail, Vincent, Bauloz, Céline (eds), *Research Handbook on International Law and Migration*, Cheltenham, Edward Elgar Publishing, 2014, p. 417 ff.

Chetail, Vincent, "Looking beyond the Rhetoric of the Refugee Crisis: The Failed Reform of the Common European Asylum System", in *European Journal of Human Rights*, N. 5, 2016, p. 584 ff.

Chetail, Vincent, De Bruycker, Philippe, Maiani, Francesco (eds), *Reforming the Common European Asylum System: The New European Refugee Law*, Leiden, Brill Nijhoff, 2016.

Christoph Safferling, Eckart Conze (eds), *The Genocide Convention Sixty Years After its Adoption*, The Hague, T.M.C. Asser Press, 2010, p. 245 ff.

Collett, Elizabeth, Fratzke, Susan, "Europe Pushes to Outsource Asylum, Again", in *Migration Policy Institute*, June 2018, available at https://www.migrationpolicy.org/news/europe-pushes-outsource-asylum-again/ (accessed on 7 October 2018).

Condorelli, Luigi, Kress, Claus, "The Rules of Attribution: General Considerations", in *The Law of International Responsibility* (J. Crawford, A. Pellet, S. Olleson eds), Oxford, Oxford University Press, 2010, p. 221 ff.

Conforti, Benedetto, "Exploring the Strasbourg Case-Law: Reflections on State Responsibility for the Breach of Positive Obligations", in *Issues of State Responsibility before International Judicial Institutions* (M. Fitzmaurice, D. Sarooshi eds), Oxford, Hart Publishing, 2004, p. 129 ff.

Corten, Olivier, Dony, Marianne, "Accord politique ou juridique: quelle est la nature du "machin" conclu entre l'UE et la Turquie en matière d'asile?", in *EU Immigration and Asylum Law and Policy*, 10 June 2016, available at http://eumigrationlawblog.eu/accord-politique-ou-juridique-quelle-est-la-nature-du-machin-conclu-entre-lue-et-la-turquie-en-matiere-dasile/ (accessed on 10 May 2018).

Corten, Olivier, Klein, Pierre, "The Limits of Complicity as a Ground for Responsibility: Lessons Learned from the Corfu Channel Case", in *The ICJ and the Evolution of International Law* (K. Bannelier, T. Christakis, S. Heathcote eds), London, Routledge, 2011, p. 314 ff.

Costello, Cathryn, "Safe Country? Says Who?", in *International Journal Refugee Law*, Vol. 28, N. 4, 2016, p. 601 ff.

Costello, Cathryn, *The Human Rights of Migrants and Refugees in European Law*, Oxford, Oxford University Press, 2016.

Crawford, James, *The International Law Commission's Articles on State Responsibility: Introduction, Text and Commentaries*, Cambridge, Cambridge University Press, 2002.

Crawford, James, *State Responsibility: The General Part*, Cambridge, Cambridge University Press, 2013.

Crépeau,François, Atak, Idil, "Global Migration Governance: Avoiding Commitments on Human Rights, Yet Tracing a Course for Cooperation", in *Netherlands Quarterly of Human Rights*, Vol. 34, N. 2, 2016, p. 113 ff.

Danisi, Carmelo, "Taking the 'Union' out of the 'EU': The EU-Turkey Statement on the Syrian Refugee Crisis as an Agreement Between States under International Law", in *European Journal of International Law: Talk!*, 20 April 2017, available at https://www.ejiltalk.org/taking-the-union-out-of-eu-the-eu-turkey-statement-on-the-syrian-refugee-crisis-as-an-agreement-between-states-under-international-law/ (accessed on 7 October 2018).

Dastyari, Azadeh, Hirsch, Asher (n.d.) "The Ring of Steel: Extraterritorial Migration Controls in Indonesia and Libya and the Complicity of Australia and Italy", in *Human Rights Law Review* (forthcoming), available at https://www.academia.edu/37586230/The_Ring_of_Steel_Extraterritorial_Migration_Controls_in_Indonesia_and_Libya_and_the_Complicity_of_Australia_and_Italy.

De Boer, Tom, "Closing Legal Black Holes: The Role of Extraterritorial Jurisdiction in Refugee Rights Protection", in *Journal of Refugee Studies*, Vol. 28, N. 1, 2014, p. 118 ff.

De Bruycker, Philippe, Foblets, Marie Claire, Maes, Maarlen (eds), *External Dimensions of EU Migration and Asylum Law and Policy / Dimensions externes du droit et de la politique d'immigration et d'asile de l'UE*, Brussels, Bruylant, 2011.

De Bruycker, Philippe, "A Happy New Year for Migration and Asylum Policy? A Critical Review of the Legal and Policy Developments in 2016 in Relation to the Crisis of the European Union", in *EU Immigration and Asylum Law and Policy*, 18 January 2017, available at http://eumigrationlawblog.eu/a-happy-new-year-for-migration-and-asylum-policy/ (accessed on 7 October 2018).

Del Guercio, Adele, "La compatibilità dei respingimenti dei migranti verso la Libia con la Convenzione europea dei diritti umani alla luce del ricorso Hirsi e altri c. Italia", in *Rassegna di diritto pubblico europeo*, Vol. 10, N. 2, 2011 p. 255 ff.

Del Guercio, Adele, *La protezione dei richiedenti asilo nel diritto internazionale ed europeo*, Napoli, Editoriale Scientifica, 2016.

Del Guercio, Adele, "La sentenza X. e X. della Corte di giustizia sul rilascio del visto umanitario: analisi critica di un'occasione persa", in *European Papers*, 2017, p. 271 ff. available at http://www.europeanpapers.eu/en/europeanforum/la-sentenza-x-e-x-della-corte-di-giustizia-sul-rilascio-del-visto-umanitario (accessed on 30 October 2018).

De Schutter, Olivier, "Globalization and Jurisdiction: Lessons from the European Convention on Human Rights", in *Baltic Yearbook of International Law* (C. Laurin ed), Leiden, Brill/Nijhoff, 2006, p. 185 ff.

De Sena, Pasquale, *La nozione di giurisdizione statale nei trattati sui diritti dell'uomo*, Torino, Giappichelli editore, 2002.

De Sena, Pasquale, "The Notion of 'Contracting Parties' Jurisdiction' in Art. 1 of the ECHR: Some Marginal Remarks on Nigro's Paper", in *The Italian Yearbook of International Law Online*, Vol. 20, 2010, p. 73 ff.

De Vittor, Francesca, "Responsabilità degli Stati e dell'Unione europea nella conclusione e nell'esecuzione di 'accordi' per il controllo extraterritoriale della migrazione", in *Diritti umani e diritto internazionale*, Vol. 12, N. 1, 2018, p. 5 ff.

De Vittor, Francesca, "Soccorso in mare e favoreggiamento dell'immigrazione irregolare: sequestro e dissequestro della nave Open Arms", in *Diritti umani e diritto internazionale*, Vol. 12, N. 2, 2018, p. 443 ff.

De Vylder, Helena, "X and X v. Belgium: A Missed Opportunity for the CJEU to Rule on the State's Obligations to Issue Humanitarian Visa for Those in Need of Protection", in *Strasbourg Observer*, 14 April 2017, available at https://strasbourgobservers.com/2017/04/14/x-and-x-v-belgium-a-missed-opportunity-for-the-cjeu-to-rule-on-the-states-obligations-to-issue-humanitarian-visa-for-those-in-need-of-protection/ (accessed on 30 October 2018).

Den Heijer, Maarten, *Europe and Extraterritorial Asylum*, Oxford, Hart Publishing, 2012.

Den Heijer, Maarten, "Issues of Shared Responsibility before the European Court of Human Rights", Shares Research Paper N. 4, 2012, available at http://www.sharesproject.nl/wp-content/uploads/2012/01/Den-Heijer-Maarten-Issues-of-Shared-Responsibility-before-the-European-Court-of-Human-Rights-ACIL-2012-041.pdf (accessed on 7 October 2018).

Den Heijer, Maarten, "Reflections on *Refoulement* and Collective Expulsion in the Hirsi Case", in *International Journal of Refugee Law*, Vol. 25, N. 2, 2013, p. 265 ff.

Den Heijer, Maarten, Lawson, Rick, "Extraterritorial Human Rights and the Concept of "Jurisdiction"", in *Global Justice, State Duties: The Extraterritorial Scope of Economic, Social and Cultural Rights in International Law* (M. Langford, W. Vandenhole, M. Sheinin, W. van Genugten eds), Cambridge, Cambridge University Press, 2013, p. 153 ff.

Den Heijer, Martin, Rijpma, Jorrit J., Spijkerboer, Thomas, "Coercion, Prohibition, and Great Expectations: The Continuing Failure of the Common European Asylum System", in *Common Market Law Review*, Vol. 53, 2016, p. 607 ff.

Den Heijer, Martin, Spijkerboer, Thomas, "Is the EU-Turkey Refugee and Migration Deal a Treaty?", in *EU Law Analysis*, 7 April 2016, available at http://eulawanalysis.blogspot.be/2016/04/is-eu-turkey-refugee-and-migration-deal.html (accessed on 10 May 2018).

De Wet, Erika, "*Complicity* in the Violations of Human Rights and Humanitarian Law by Incumbent Governments through Direct Military Assistance on Request", in *International and Comparative Law Quarterly*, Vol. 67, N. 2, 2018, p. 287 ff.

Di Filippo, Marcello, "The Allocation of Competence in Asylum Procedures under EU Law: The Need to Take the Dublin Bull by the Horns", in *Revista de Derecho Comunitario Europeo*, Vol. 22, N. 59, 2018, p. 41 ff.

Di Filippo, Marcello, "Unione europea e flussi migratori, o del tramonto dello spirito comunitario: considerazioni a margine del Consiglio europeo del 28–29 giugno 2018", in *SIDIBlog*, 9 July 2018, available at http://www.sidiblog.org/author/marcello-di-filippo/ (accessed on 7 October 2018).

Dominice, Christian, "Attribution of Conduct to Multiple States and the Implication of a State in the Act of Another State", in *The Law of International Responsibility* (J. Crawford, A. Pellet, S. Olleson eds), Oxford, Oxford University Press, 2010, p. 281 ff.

Duffy, Helen, "The Practice of Shared Responsibility in relation to Detention and Interrogation Abroad: The 'Extraordinary Rendition' Programme", in *SHARES Research Paper* 78, 2016, p. 16, available at http://www.sharesproject.nl/publication/the-practice-of-shared-responsibility-in-relation-to-detention-and-interrogation-abroad-the-extraordinary-rendition-programme/ (accessed on 7 October 2018).

Favilli, Chiara, "La cooperazione UE-Turchia per contenere il flusso dei migranti e richiedenti asilo: obiettivo riuscito?", in *Diritti umani e diritto internazionale*, Vol. 10, N. 2, 2016 p. 405 ff.

Favilli, Chiara, "Visti umanitari e protezione internazionale: così vicini così lontani", in *Diritti umani e Diritto internazionale*, 2017, p. 553 ff., available at http://www.sidi-isil.org/wp-content/uploads/2017/04/Osservatorio-Favilli-per-SIDI.pdf (accessed on 30 October 2018).

Favilli, Chiara, *"L'Unione che protegge e l'Unione che respinge.* Progressi, contraddizioni *e* paradossi del sistema europeo di asilo", in *Questione Giustizia*, 2018, p. 28 ff, available at http://questionegiustizia.it/rivista/2018/2/l-unione-che-protegge-e-l-unione-che-respinge-prog_532.php (accessed on 30 November 2018).

Fernández Arribas, Gloria, "The EU-Turkey Agreement: A Controversial Attempt at Patching up a Major Problem", in *European Papers*, 2016, available at http://europeanpapers.eu/en/system/files/pdf_version/EP_EF_2016_I_040_Gloria_Fernandez_Arribas_2.pdf (accessed on 7 October 2018).

Fernández Arribas, Gloria, "The EU-Turkey Statement, the Treaty-Making Process and Competent Organs. Is the Statement an International Agreement?", in *European Papers*, 2017, p. 303 ff., available at http://www.europeanpapers.eu/fr/system/files/pdf_version/EP_EF_2017_I_012_Gloria_Fernandez_Arribas_1.pdf (accessed on 7 October 2018).

Ferri, Federico, "Convergenza delle politiche migratorie e di cooperazione allo sviluppo dell'Unione Europea e accordi con Stati terzi", in *Diritto, Immigrazione e Cittadinanza*, Vol. 3, N. 3–4, 2016, p. 36 ff.

Ferri, Federico, "Il Codice di condotta per le ONG e i diritti dei migranti: fra diritto internazionale e politiche europee", in *Diritti umani e diritto internazionale*, 2018, p. 189 ff.

Fink, Melanie, "A 'Blind Spot' in the Framework of International Responsibility? Third-Party Responsibility for Human Rights Violations: The Case of Frontex", in *Human Rights and the Dark Side of Globalisation* (T. Gammeltoft-Hansen, J. Vedsted-Hansen eds), London and New York, Routledge, 2017.

Fink, *Melanie,* Gombeer, Kristof, Rijpma, *Jorrit,* "In Search of a Safe Harbour for the Aquarius: the Troubled Waters of International and EU Law", in *EU Immigration and Asylum Law and Policy*, 9 July 2018, available at http://eumigrationlawblog.eu/in-search-of-a-safe-harbour-for-the-aquarius-the-troubled-waters-of-international-and-eu-law/ (accessed on 7 October 2018).

Fischer-Lescano, Andreas, Löhr, Tillman, Tohidipur, Timo, "Border Controls at Sea: Requirements under International Human Rights and Refugee Law", in *International Journal of Refugee Law*, Vol. 21, N. 2, 2009, p. 256 ff.

Focarelli, Carlo, *Trattato di diritto internazionale*, Torino, Utet, 2015.

Forlati, Serena, "Violazione dell'obbligo di prevenire il genocidio e riparazione nell'affare Bosnia-Erzegovina c. Serbia", in *Rivista di diritto internazionale*, 2007, p. 425 ff.

Forlati, Serena, "Le contenu des obligations primaires de diligence: prévention, cessation, repression...?", in *Le standard de due diligence et la responsabilité internationale-Journée d'études franco-italienne du Mans* (S. Cassella ed), Paris, Pedone, 2018, p. 39 ff.

Francis, Angus, "Bringing Protection Home: Healing the Schism Between International Obligations and National Safeguards Created by Extraterritorial Processing", in *International Journal of Refugee Law*, Vol. 20, N. 2, 2008, p. 273 ff.

Frelick, Bill, Kysel, Ian M., Podkul, Jennifer, "The Impact of Externalization of Migration Controls on the Rights of Asylum Seekers and Other Migrants", in *Journal on Migration and Human Security*, Vol. 4, N. 4, 2016, p. 190 ff.

Gaja, Giorgio, "Art. 1", in *Commentario alla Convenzione europea per la salvaguardia dei diritti dell'uomo* (S. Bartole, B. Conforti, G. Raimondi eds), Padova, Cedam, 2001, p. 28.

Gaja, Giorgio, "Do States Have a Duty to Ensure Compliance with Obligations *Erga Omnes* by Other States?", in *International Responsibility Today: Essays in Memory of Oscar Schachter* (M. Ragazzi ed), Leiden, Martinus Nijhoff, 2005, p. 8 ff.

Gaja, Giorgio, "Interpreting Articles Adopted by the International Law Commission", in *British Yearbook of International Law*, Vol. 85, N. 1, 2015, p. 10 ff.

Gammeltoft-Hansen, Thomas, *Access to Asylum: International Refugee Law and the Globalisation of Migration Control*, Cambridge, Cambridge University Press, 2011.

Gammeltoft-Hansen, Thomas, "The Externalisation of European Migration Control and the Reach of International Refugee Law", in *The First Decade of EU Migration and Asylum Law* (E. Guild, P. Minderhoud eds), Leiden, Martinus Nijhoff, 2012, p. 273 ff.

Gammeltoft-Hansen, Thomas, Hathaway, James C., "Non-Refoulement in a World of Cooperative Deterrence", in *Columbia Journal of Transnational Law*, Vol. 53, N. 2, 2015, p. 235 ff.

Gammeltoft-Hansen, Thomas, Vedsted-Hansen, Jens (eds), *Human Rights and the Dark Side of Globalisation*, Routledge, London and New York, 2017.

Gatta, Francesco Luigi, "Detention of Migrants with the View to Implement the EU-Turkey Statement: The Court of Strasbourg (Un)Involved in the EU

Migration Policy", in *Cahiers de l'EDEM*, 2018, available at https://uclouvain. be/fr/instituts-recherche/juri/cedie/actualites/judgment-of-the-european-court-of-human-rights-in-the-case-j-r-and-others-v-greece-appl-no-22696-16. html (accessed on 7 October 2018).

Gattini, Andrea, "Breach of the Obligation to Prevent and Reparation Thereof in the ICJ's Genocide Judgment", in *European Journal of International Law*, N. 4, 2007, available at http://www.ejil.org/pdfs/18/4/237.pdf (accessed on 7 October 2018).

Gauci, Jean-Pierre, "Back to Old Tricks? Italian Responsibility for Returning People to Libya", in *European Journal of International Law: Talk!*, 6 June 2017, available at https://www.ejiltalk.org/back-to-old-tricks-italian-responsibility-for-returning-people-to-libya/ (accessed on 7 October 2018).

Gestri, Marco, "Eunavfor Med: Fighting Migrant Smuggling under UN Security Council Resolution 2240 (2015)", in *Italian Yearbook of International Law*, Vol. 25, 2016, p. 21 ff.

Gibney, Mark, Tomasevski, Katarina, Vedsted-Hansen, Jens, "Transnational State Responsibility for Violations of Human Rights", in *Harvard Human Rights Journal*, Vol. 12, 1999, p. 267 ff.

Gibney, Mark, "Genocide and State Responsibility", in *Human Rights Law Review*, Vol. 7, N. 4, 2007, p. 760 ff.

Giuffré, Mariagiulia, "State Responsibility Beyond Borders: What Legal Basis for Italy's Pushbacks to Libya?", in *International Journal If Refugee Law*, Vol. 24, N. 4, 2012, p. 692 ff.

Giuffré, Mariagiulia, "Watered-Down Rights on the High Seas: Hirsi Jamaa and Others v Italy", in *International & Comparative Law Quarterly*, Vol. 61, N. 3, 2012, p. 728 ff.

Giuffré, Mariagiulia, "From Turkey to Libya: The EU Migration Partnership from Bad to Worse", in *Eurojus*, March 2017, available at http://rivista.eurojus.it/from-turkey-to-libya-the-eu-migration-partnership-from-bad-to-worse/ (accessed on 7 October 2018).

Goodwin-Gill, Guy S., "Safe Country? Says Who?", in *International Journal oh Refugee Law*, Vol. 4, N. 2, 1992, p. 248 ff.

Goodwin-Gill, Guy S., "The Extraterritorial Processing of Claims to Asylum or Protection: The Legal Responsibilities of States and International Organisations", in *University of Technology Sydney Law Review*, N. 9, 2007, p. 26 ff.

Goodwin-Gill, Guy S., McAdam, Jane, *The Refugee in International Law* (3rd edn), Oxford, Oxford University Press, 2007.

Goodwin-Gill, Guy S., "The Right to Seek Asylum: Interception at Sea and the Principle of Non-Refoulement", in *International Journal of Refugee Law*, Vol. 23, N. 3, 2011, p. 443 ff.

Goodwin-Gill, Guy S., "YLS Sale Symposium: The Globalization of High Seas Interdiction. Sale's Legacy and Beyond", in *OpinioJuris*, 16 March 2014, available at http://opiniojuris.org/2014/03/16/yale-sale-symposium-globalization-high-seas-interdiction-sales-legacy-beyond (accessed on 7 October 2018).

Graefrath, Bernhard, "Complicity in the Law of International Responsibility", in *Revue Belge de Droit International*, Vol. 29, N. 2, 1996,, p. 370 ff.

Griebel, Jörn, Plücken, Milan, "New Developments Regarding the Rules of Attribution? The International Court of Justice's Decision in Bosnia v. Serbia" in *Leiden Journal of International Law*, Vol. 21, N. 3, 2008, p. 601 ff.

Guild, Elspeth, Minderhoud, Paul (eds), *The First Decade of EU Migration and Asylum Law*, Leiden, Nijhoff, 2012.

Guild, Elspeth, "The Dark Side of Globalization: Do EU Border Controls Contribute to Death in the Mediterranean?", in *Human Rights and the Dark Side of Globalisation* (T. Gammeltoft-Hansen, J. Vedsted-Hansen eds), London and New York, Routledge, 2017, p. 314 ff.

Guild, Espelth, Carrera, Sergio, "Offshore Processing of Asylum Applications: Out of Sight, Out of Mind?", in *CEPS Commentary*, 27 January 2017, available at https://www.ceps.eu/publications/offshore-processing-asylum-applications-out-sight-out-mind (accessed on 7 October 2018).

Hailbronner, Kay, Thym, Daniel (ed), *EU Immigration and Asylum Law, A Commentary*, (2nd Ed.), München, Oxford, Baden, C.H. Beck/Hart/Nomos, 2016.

Hakimi, Monica, "State Bystander Responsibility", in *European Journal of International Law*, Vol. 21, N. 2, 2010, p. 341 ff.

Hathaway, James C., "The Emerging Politics of Non-Entree", in *Refugees*, Vol. 91, 1992, p 39 ff.

Hathaway, James C., *The Rights if Refugees under International Law*, Cambridge, Cambridge University Press, 2005.

Hirsch, Asher, "The Borders Beyond the Border: Australia's Extraterritorial Migration Controls", in *Refugee Survey Quarterly*, Vol. 36, N. 3, 2017, p. 36 ff.

Idriz, Narin, "Taking the EU-Turkey Deal to Court?", in *Verfassungsblog*, 20 December 2017, available at https://verfassungsblog.de/taking-the-eu-turkey-deal-to-court/, (accessed on 28 March 2018).

Ippolito, Francesca, Trevisanut, Seline, *Migration in the Mediterranean. Mechanism of International Cooperation*, Cambridge, Cambridge University Press, 2016.

Jackson, Miles, *Complicity in International Law*, Oxford, Oxford University Press, 2015.

Jackson, Miles, "Freeing *Soering*: The ECHR, State Complicity in Torture and Jurisdiction", in *European Journal of International Law*, Vol. 27, N. 3, 2016, p. 817 ff.

Jensen, Ulla Iben, *Humanitarian Visas: Options or Obligations?* Study for the LIBE Committee of the European Parliament, 2014, available at http://www.epgencms.europarl.europa.eu/cmsdata/upload/eb469bdf-0e31-40bb-8c75-8db410ab13fc/Session_2_-_Study_Humanitarian_visas.pdf, (accessed on 7 October 2018).

Klein, Natalie S., "Multilateral Disputes and the Doctrine of Necessary Parties in the East Timor Case", in *Yale Journal of International Law*, Vol. 21, N. 2, 1996, p. 305 ff.

Klug, Anja, Howe, Tim, "The Concept of State Jurisdiction and the Applicability of the Non-Refoulement Principle to Extraterritorial Interception Measures", in *Extraterritorial Immigration Control: Legal Challenges* (B. Ryan and V. Mitsilegas eds), Leiden, Brill-Nijhoff, 2010.

Kneebone, Susan, "The Pacific Plan: The Provision of 'Effective Protection'", in *International Journal of Refugee Law*, Vol.18, N. 3–4, 2006, p. 696 ff.

Koh, Harold, "The 'Haiti Paradigm' in United States Human Rights Policy", in *Yale Law Journal*, Vol. 103, N. 8, 1994, p. 2391 ff.

Labayle, Henri, De Bruycker, Philippe, "L'accord Union européenne-Turquie: faux semblant ou marché dedupes?", in *Réseau Universitaire européen du droit de l'Espace de liberté, sécurité et justice*, 23 March 2016, available at http://www.gdr-elsj.eu/2016/03/23/asile/laccord-union-europeenne-turquie-faux-semblant-ou-marche-de-dupes/ (accessed on 7 October 2018).

Lagrange, Evelyne, "L'application de la Convention de Rome à des actes accomplis par les Etats parties en dehors du territoire national", in *Revue générale de droit international public*, Vol. 112, N. 3, 2008, p. 521 ff.

Lanovoy, Vladyslav, "Complicity in an International Wrongful Act", SHARES Research Paper 38, 2014, available at http://www.sharesproject.nl/wp-content/uploads/2014/03/SHARES-RP-38-final.pdf (accessed on 7 October 2018).

Larsen, Kjetil Mujezinović, *The Human Rights Treaty Obligations of Peacekeepers*, Cambridge, Cambridge University Press, 2012.

Lauro, Alessandro, "Il conflitto fra poteri dello Stato e la forma di governo parlamentare: a margine delle ordinanze 163 e 181 del 2018", in *Quaderni Costituzionali*, 2018, available at http://www.forumcostituzionale.it/wordpress/wp-content/uploads/2018/10/nota_163_181_2018_lauro.pdf (accessed on 7 October 2018).

Lauterpacht, Elihu, Bethlehem, Daniel, "The Scope and Content of the Principle of Non-refoulement: Opinion", in *Refugee Protection in International Law: UNHCR's Global Consultations on International Protection* (E. Feller, V. Turk, and F. Nicholson eds), Cambridge, Cambridge University Press, 2003, available at http://www.refworld.org/docid/470a33af0.html (accessed on 7 October 2018).

Lavenex, Sandra, "Shifting Up and Out: The Foreign Policy of European Immigration Control", in *West European Politics*, 2006, p. 329 ff. available at https://www.eui.eu/Documents/DepartmentsCentres/AcademyofEuropeanLaw/CourseMaterialsUL/UL2010/BoswellReading4.pdf, (accessed on 7 October 2018).

Legomsky, Stephen H., "The USA and the Caribbean Interdiction Program", in *International Journal of Refugee Law*, Vol. 18, N. 3–4, 2006, p. 680 ff.

Lehmann, Julian, "The Use of Force against People Smugglers: Conflicts with Refugee Law and Human Rights Law", in *European Journal of International Law: Talk!*, available at http://www.ejiltalk.org/the-use-of-force-against-people-smugglers-conflicts-with-refugee-law-and-human-rights-law/ (accessed on 30 November 2018).

Lenzerini, Federico, "Il principio del "non-refoulement" dopo la sentenza "Hirsi" della Corte europea dei diritti dell'uomo", in *Rivista di diritto internazionale*, Vol. 95, N. 3, 2012, p. 721 ff.

Liguori, Anna, "La Corte europea dei diritti dell'uomo condanna l'Italia per i respingimenti verso la Libia del 2009: il caso Hirsi", in *Rivista di diritto internazionale*, Vol. 95, N. 2, 2012, p. 415 ff.

Liguori, Anna, "Some Observations on the Legal Responsibility of States and International Organizations in the Extraterritorial Processing of Asylum Claims", in *Italian Yearbook of International Law*, Vol. XXV, 2016, p. 135 ff.

Liguori, Anna, "Extraordinary Renditions nella giurisprudenza della Corte europea dei diritti umani: il caso Abu Omar", in *Rivista di diritto internazionale*, Vol. 99, N. 3, 2016, p. 777 ff.

Liguori, Anna, "The 2017 Italy-Libya Memorandum and Its Consequences", in *Migration in the Mediterranean Area and the Challenges for Hosting European Society* (G. Cataldi, M. Pace, A. Liguori eds), Napoli, Editoriale scientifica, 2017, p. 215 ff.

Limone, Luigi, "Today's Court (Non) Decision on the (Non) EU "deal"? with Turkey", in *European Area of Freedom Security & Justice FREE Group*, 1 March 2017, available at https://free-group.eu/2017/03/01/the-todays-court-non-decision-on-the-non-eu-deal-with-turkey/ (accessed on 7 October 2018).

Limone, Luigi, " EU-Afghanistan'Joint Way Forward on Migration Issues': Another 'Surrealist' EU Legal Text?", in *European Area of Freedom, Security & Justice*, 11 April 2017, available at https://free-group.eu/2017/04/11/euafghanistan-joint-way-forward-on-migration-issues-anothersurrealist-eu-legal-text/ (accessed on 5 December 2018).

Lowe, Vaughan, *International Law*, Oxford, Oxford University Press, 2007.

Maccanico Yasha, "Morocco: Wherever EU Immigration Policy Rears Its Ugly Head, Violence and Abuses Follow", available at http://www.state watch.org/analyses/no-334-morocco-migration-expulsions.pdf (accessed on 30 October 2018).

Mackenzie-Gray Scott, Richard, "Torture in Libya and Questions of EU Member State Complicity", in *European Journal of International Law: Talk!*, 11 January 2018, available at https://www.ejiltalk.org/torture-in-libya-and-questions-of-eu-member-state-complicity/ (accessed on 7 October 2018).

Maiani, Francesco, "'Regional Disembarkation Platforms' and 'Controlled Centres': Lifting The Drawbridge, Reaching out Across The Mediterranean, or Going Nowhere?", in *EU Immigration and Asylum Law and Policy*, 18 September 2018, available at http://eumigrationlawblog.eu/regional-disembarkation-platforms-and-controlled-centres-lifting-the-drawbridge-reaching-out-across-the-mediterranean-or-going-nowhere/ (accessed on 7 October 2018).

Mancini, Marina, "Italy's New Migration Control Policy: Stemming the Flow of Migrants from Libya Without Regard for Their Human Rights", in *Italian Yearbook of International Law*, Vol. XXVII, 2018, p. 259 ff.

Mann, Itamar, Moreno-Lax, Violeta, Shatz, Omer, "Time to Investigate European Agents for Crimes against Migrants in Libya", in *European*

Journal of International Law: Talk!, 29 March 2018, available at https://www.ejiltalk.org/time-to-investigate-european-agents-for-crimes-against-migrants-in-libya/ (accessed on 7 October 2018).

Marchegiani, Maura, Marotti, Loris, "L'accordo tra l'Unione europea e la Turchia per la gestione dei flussi migratori: cronaca di una morte annunciata?", in *Diritto, Immigrazione e Cittadinanza*, Vol. 1–2, 2016, p. 59 ff.

Marinai, Simone, "The Interception and Rescue at Sea of Asylum Seekers in the Light of the New EU Legal Framework", in *Revista de Derecho Comunitario Europeo*, December 2016, p. 901 ff.

Markard, Nora, "The Right to Leave by Sea: Legal Limits on EU Migration Control by Third Countries", in *European Journal of Migration and Law*, Vol. 27, N. 3, 2016, p. 591 ff.

McAdam, Jane, "Australia and Asylum Seekers", in *International Journal of Refugee Law*, Vol. 25, N. 3, 2013, p. 435 ff.

McAdam, Jane, "Migrating Laws? The 'Plagiaristic Dialogue' between Europe and Australia", in *The Global Reach of European Refugee Law* (H. Lambert, J. McAdam, M. Fullerton eds), Cambridge, Cambridge University Press, 2013, p. 25 ff.

Messineo, Francesco, "Yet Another Mala Figura: Italy Breached Non-Refoulement Obligations by Intercepting Migrants' Boats at Sea, Says ECtHR", in *European Journal of International Law: Talk!*, 24 February 2012, available at https://www.ejiltalk.org/yet-another-mala-figura-italy-breached-non-refoulement-obligations-by-intercepting-migrants-boats-at-sea-says-ecthr/ (accessed on 7 October 2018).

Milanovic, Marko, *Extraterritorial Application of Human Rights Treaties: Law, Principles, and Policy*, Oxford, Oxford University Press, 2011.

Milanovic, Marko, "Al-Skeini and Al-Jedda in Strasbourg", in *European Journal of International Law*, Vol. 23, N. 1, 2012, p. 121 ff.

Milanovic, Marko, "Grand Chamber Judgment in Catan and Others", in *European Journal of International Law Talk!*, 21 October 2012, available at https://www.ejiltalk.org/grand-chamber-judgment-in-catan-and-others/ (accessed on 7 October 2018).

Moreno-Lax, Violeta, "Hirsi v. Italy or the Strasbourg Court versus Extraterritorial Migration Control?", in *Human Rights Law Review*, Vol. 12, N. 3, 4 October 2012, p. 574 ff.

Moreno-Lax, Violeta, Costello, Cathryn, "The Extraterritorial Application of the EU Charter of Fundamental Rights: From Territoriality to Facticity, the Effectiveness Model", in *The EU Charter of Fundamental Rights: A Commentary* (S. Peers, T. Hervey, J. Kenner, A. Ward eds), Oxford, Hart Publishing, 2014, p. 1680 ff.

Moreno-Lax, Violeta, "The External Dimension of the Common European Asylum System", in *EU Immigration and Asylum Law* (S. Peers, V. Moreno-Lax V., M. Garlick M. and E. Guild eds), Vol. 3, 2nd Ed., Leiden/Boston, Brill - Nijhoff, 2015, p. 617–674.

Moreno-Lax, Violeta, *Accessing Asylum Europe: Extraterritorial Border Controls and Refugee Rights Under EU Law*, Oxford, Oxford University Press, 2017.

Moreno-Lax, Violeta, "Asylum Visas as an Obligation under EU Law: Case PPU C-638/16 X, X v État belge" (Part. I-II), in *EU Immigration and Asylum Law and Policy*, 16 February 2017, available at http://eumigrationlawblog. eu/asylum-visas-as-an-obligation-under-eu-law-case-ppu-c-63816-x-x-v-etat-belge/ (accessed on 30 October 2018).

Moreno-Lax, Violeta, Giuffré, Mariagiulia, "The Rise of Consensual Containment: From 'Contactless Control' to 'Contactless Responsibility' for Forced Migration Flows", in *Research Handbook on International Refugee Law* (Juss ed), Cheltenham, 31 March 2017, available at https://papers.ssrn. com/sol3/papers.cfm?abstract_id=3009331, (accessed on 7 October 2018).

Morgese, Giuseppe, "Recenti iniziative dell'Unione europea per affrontare la crisi dei rifugiati", in *Diritto immigrazione e cittadinanza*, N. 3–4, 2015, p. 15 ff.

Moynihan, Harriet, "Aiding and Assisting: The Mental Element under Article 16 of the International Law Commission's Articles on State Responsibility", in *International & Comparative Law Quarterly*, Vol. 67, N. 2, 2017, p. 455 ff.

Nahapetian, Kate, "Confronting State Complicity in International Law", in *UCLA Journal of International Law and Foreign Affairs*, Vol. 7, 2002, p. 99 ff.

Nagy, Boldizsár, "Renegade in the Club – Hungary's Resistance to EU Efforts in the Asylum Field", in *Osteuropa-recht*, 2017, p. 413 ff.

Napoletano, Nicola, "La condanna dei 'respingimenti' operati dall'Italia verso la Libia da parte della Corte europea dei diritti umani: molte luci e qualche ombra", in *Diritti umani e diritto internazionale*, Vol. 6, N. 2, 2012, p. 436 ff.

Nascimbene, Bruno, "Refugees, the European Union and the 'Dublin System'. The Reasons for a Crisis", in *European Papers*, 2016, p. 101 ss., available at http://europeanpapers.eu/it/e-journal/refugees-european-union-and-dublin-system-reasons-crisis (accessed on 15 November 2018).

Nigro, Raffaella, "Giurisdizione e obblighi positivi degli Stati parti della Convenzione europea dei diritti dell'uomo: il caso Ilascu", in *Rivista di diritto internazionale*, Vol. 88, N. 2, 2005, p. 413 ff.

Nigro, Raffaella, "The Notion of 'Jurisdiction' in Article 1: Future Scenarios for the Extra-Territorial Application of the European Convention on Human Rights" in *The Italian Yearbook of International Law Online*, Vol. 20, N. 1, January 2010, p. 9 ff., available at http://www.sidi-isil.org/wp-content/ uploads/2010/12/Yearbook2011_nigro.pdf (accessed on 5 December 2018).

Noll, Gregor, "Visions of the Exceptional: Legal and Theoretical Issues Raised by Transit Processing Centres and Protection Zones", in *European Journal of Migration and Law*, Vol. 5, N. 3, January 2003, p. 303 ff.

Nollkaemper, André, "Issues of Shared Responsibility before the International Court of Justice", *Research Project on Shared Responsibility in International Law*, Amsterdam, Amsterdam Centre for International Law, 2011. Shares Research Paper no. 2011-01, available at http://www.shares project.nl/wp-content/uploads/2011/04/01-Nollkaemper-Issues-of-Shared-Responsibility-before-the-International-Court-of-Justice1.pdf (accessed on 7 October 2018).

Nollkaemper, André, "The ECtHR Finds Macedonia Responsible in Connection with Torture by the CIA, but on What Basis?", in *European Journal of*

International Law: Talk!, 24 December 2012, available at http://www.ejiltalk. org/the-ecthrfinds-macedonia-responsible-in-connection-withtorture-by-the-cia-but-on-what-basis/ (accessed on 7 October 2018).

Nollkaemper, André, Dov Jacobs, "Shared Responsibility in International Law: A Conceptual Framework", in *Michigan Journal if International Law*, Vol. 34, N. 2, 2013, p. 359 ff.

Nollkaemper André, Plakokefalos, Ilias (eds) *Principles of Shared Responsibility in International Law: An Appraisal of the State of the Art*, Cambridge, Cambridge University Press, 2014.

Nolte, Georg, Aust, Helmut Philippe, "Equivocal Helpers: Complicit States, Mixed Messages and International Law", in *International and Comparative Law Quarterly*, Vol. 58, N. 1, 2009, p. 1 ff.

O'Boyle, Michael, "The European Convention on Human Rights and extra-territorial jurisdiction: a comment on 'life after Bankovic'", in *Extraterritorial Application of human rights treaties* (Coomans and Kamminga eds), Antwerpen, Intersentia, 2004, p. 125 ff.

Orakhelashvili, Alexander, "Division of Reparation between Responsible Entities", in *The Law of International Responsibility* (J. Crawford, A. Pellet, S. Olleson eds), Oxford, Oxford University Press, 2010, p. 651.

Padelletti, Maria Luisa, *Pluralità di Stati nel fatto illecito internazionale*, Giuffrè, Milano, 1990.

Palchetti, Paolo, "State Responsibility for Complicity in Genocide", in *The UN Genocide Convention - A Commentary* (P. Gaeta ed), Oxford, Oxford University Press, 2009.

Palladino, Rossana, "Nuovo quadro di partenariato dell'Unione europea per la migrazione e profili di responsabilità dell'Italia (e dell'Unione europea) in riferimento al caso libico", in *Freedom, Security & Justice: European Legal Studies*, 2018, p. 104 ff., available at http://www.fsjeurostudies.eu/files/ FSJ.2018.II.Palladino_DEF5.pdf (accessed on 7 October 2018).

Palm, Anja, "The Italy-Libya Memorandum of Understanding: The Baseline of a Policy Approach Aimed at Closing All Doors to Europe?", in *EU Immigration and Asylum Law and Policy*, 2 October 2017, available at http:// eumigrationlawblog.eu/the-italy-libya-memorandum-of-understanding-the-baseline-of-a-policy-approach-aimed-at-closing-all-doors-to-europe/ (accessed on 7 October 2018).

Papanicolopulu, Irini, "Immigrazione irregolare via mare, tutela della vita umana e organizzazioni non governative", in *Diritto, Immigrazione e Cittadinanza*, N. 3, 2017, p. 1 ff., available at https://www.dirittoimmigrazionecittadinanza. it/archivio-saggi-commenti/saggi/fascicolo-n-3-2017/162-immigrazione-irregolare-via-mare-tutela-della-vita-umana-e-organizzazioni-non-governative-1/file (accessed on 7 October 2018).

Papastavridis, Efthymios, "EUNAVFOR MED Operation Sophia and the Question of Jurisdiction over Transnational Organized Crime at Sea", in *Questions of International Law*, 5 August 2016, p. 19 ff., available at http:// www.qil-qdi.org/eunavfor-med-operation-sophia-question-jurisdiction-transnational-organized-crime-sea/ (accessed on 7 October 2018).

Papastavridis, Efthymios, "Recent Non-Entrée Policies in the Central Mediterranean and Their Legality: A New Form of Refoulement?", in *Diritti umani e diritto internazionale*, Vol. 12, N. 3, 2018. p. 493 ff.

Pascale, Giuseppe, "«Esternalizzazione» delle frontiere in chiave antimigratoria e responsabilità internazionale dell'Italia e dell'UE per complicità nelle gross violations dei diritti umani commesse in Libia", in *Studi sull'integrazione europea*, Vol. XIII, 2018, p. 413 ff.

Paternello, Marco, "Dissequestrata la nave Open Arms: soccorrere i migranti non è reato", 19 April 2018, available at http://questionegiustizia.it/articolo/dissequestrata-la-nave-open-arms-soccorrere-i-migranti-non-e-reato_19-04-2018.php (accessed on 7 October 2018).

Peers, Steve, *EU Justice and Home Affairs Law* (3rd Ed.), Oxford, Oxford University Press, 2012.

Peers, Steve, "Do Potential Asylum-Seekers Have the Right to a Schengen Visa?", in *EU Law Analysis*, 20 January 2014, available at http://eulaw analysis.blogspot.com/2014/01/do-potential-asylum-seekers-have-right. html (accessed on 30 October 2018).

Peers, Steve, Moreno-Lax, Violeta, Garlick, Madeline, Guild, Elspeth (eds), *EU Immigration and Asylum Law* (Vol. 3, 2nd Ed.), Leiden/Boston, Brill - Nijhoff, 2015.

Peers, Steve, "The Dublin III Regulation", in *EU Immigration and Asylum Law* (S. Peers, V. Moreno-Lax, M. Garlick, E. Guild eds), Vol. 3, 2nd Ed., Leiden/Boston, Brill - Nijhoff, 2015, p. 345 ff.

Peers, Steve, "The Draft EU/Turkey Deal on Migration and Refugees: Is It legal?", *EU Law Analysis*, 16 March 2016, available at http://eulawanalysis. blogspot.be/2016/03/the-draft-euturkey-deal-on-migration.html (accessed on 30 October 2018).

Peers, Steve, Roman, Emanuela, "The EU, Turkey and the Refugee Crisis: What Could Possibly Go Wrong?", in *EU Law Analysis*, 05 February 2016, http://eulawanalysis.blogspot.com/2016/02/the-eu-turkey-and-refugee-crisis-what.html (accessed on 30 October 2018).

Peers, Steve, "The Final EU/Turkey Refugee Deal: A Legal Assessment", *EU Law Analysis*, 18 March 2016, available at http://eulawanalysis.blogspot. com/2016/03/the-final-euturkey-refugee-deal-legal.html (accessed on 30 October 2018).

Picone, Paolo, "Obblighi *erga omnes* e codificazione della responsabilità degli Stati", in *Rivista di diritto internazionale*, Vol. 88, N. 4, 2005, p. 893 ff.

Pijnenburg, Annick, "Is N.D. and N.T. v. Spain the New Hirsi?", in *European Journal of International Law: Talk!*, 17 October 2017, available at https://www. ejiltalk.org/is-n-d-and-n-t-v-spain-the-new-hirsi/ (accessed on 7 October 2018).

Pijnenburg, Annick, "JR and Others v Greece: What Does the Court (Not) Say About the EU-Turkey Statement?", in *Strasbourg Observer*, 21 February 2018, available at https://strasbourgobservers.com/2018/02/21/jr-and-others-v-greece-what-does-the-court-not-say-about-the-eu-turkey-statement (accessed on 7 October 2018).

Pisillo Mazzeschi, Riccardo, "Responsabilité de l'État pour violation des obligations positives relatives aux droits de l'homme", in *Recueil des Cours de l'Académie de Droit International de La Haye*, Vol. 333, 2008, Leiden/ Boston, Martinus Nijhoff Publishers, 2009, p. 175 ff.

Pisillo Mazzeschi, Riccardo, "Le chemin étrange de la due diligence: d'un concept mystérieux à un concept surévalué", in *Le standard de due diligence et la responsabilité internationale-Journée d'études franco-italienne du Mans* (S. Cassella ed), Paris, Pedone, 2018, p. 323 ff.

Puma, Giuseppe, *Complicità di Stati nell'illecito internazionale*, Torino, Giappichelli, 2018.

Quigley, John, "Complicity in International Law: A New Direction in the Law of State Responsibility", in *The British Yearbook of International Law*, Vol. 57, N. 1, 1986, p. 77 ff.

Raimondo, Giulia, "Visti umanitari: il caso X e X contro Belgio, C-638/16 PPU", in *Sidiblog*, 1 May 2017, available at http://www.sidiblog.org/2017/05/01/visti-umanitari-il-caso-x-e-x-contro-belgio-c%E2%80%9163816-ppu/ (accessed on 30 October 2018).

Ramacciotti, Martina, "Sulla utilità di un codice di condotta per le organizzazioni non governative impegnate in attività di search and rescue (SAR)", in *Rivista di diritto internazionale*, Vol. 101, N. 1, 2018, p. 213 ff.

Rijpma, Jorrit, "Hybrid Agencification in the Area of Freedom, Security and Justice and its Inherent Tensions: The Case of Frontex", in *The Agency Phenomenon in the European Union: Emergence, Institutionalisation and Everyday Decision-Making* (M. Busuioc, M. Groenleer, J. Trondal eds), Manchester, Manchester University Press, 2012, p. 84 ff.

Rijpma, Jorrit, "External Migration and Asylum Management: Accountability for Executive Action Outside EU-territory", in *European Papers*, Vol. 2, N. 2, 2017, p. 571 ff., available at http://www.europeanpapers.eu/en/system/files/pdf_version/EP_eJ_2017_2_7_Article_Jorrit_J_Rijpma.pdf (accessed on 30 October 2018).

Rijpma, Jorrit, Cremona, Marise, "The Extra-Territorialisation of EU Migration Policies and the Rule of Law", in *European University Institute*, Working Paper Series, no. 1, 2007.

Rizzo, Alfredo, "La dimensione esterna dello spazio di libertà, sicurezza e giustizia. Sviluppi recenti e sfide aperte", in *Freedom, Security & Justice: European Legal Studies*, N. 1, 2017, p. 147 ff., available at http://www.fsjeuro studies.eu/files/2017.1.-FSJ_Rizzo_8.pdf, (accessed on 7 October 2018).

Roman, Emanuela, "L'accordo UE-Turchia: le criticità di un accordo a tutti i costi", *SIDIBlog*, 21 March 2016, available at http://www.sidiblog.org/2016/03/21/laccordo-ueturchia-le-criticita-di-un-accordo-a-tutti-i-costi/ (accessed on 7 October 2018).

Ronzitti, Natalino, "Italia-Libia: il Trattato di Bengasi e la sua effettiva rilevanza", in *Affari Internazionali Blog*, 14 July 2018, available at http://www.affarinternazionali.it/2018/07/italia-libia-trattato-bengasi/ (accessed on 7 October 2018).

Rozakis, Christos, "The Territorial Scope of Human Rights Obligations: The Case of the European Convention on Human Rights", in *The Status of International Treaties on Human Rights*, Strasbourg, Council of Europe Publishing, 2005, p. 70 ff.

Saccucci, Andrea, "La giurisdizione esclusiva dello Stato della bandiera sulle imbarcazioni impegnate in operazioni di soccorso umanitario in alto mare: il caso della Iuventa", in *Rivista di diritto internazionale*, Vol. 101, N. 1, 2018, p. 223 ff.

Salerno, Francesco, "L'obbligo internazionale di non-refoulement dei richiedenti asilo", in *Diritti umani e diritto internazionale*, Vol. 4, N. 4, 2010, p. 487 ff.

Savino, Mario, "The Diciotti Affair: Beyond the Populist Farce", in *Verfassungsblog*, 2 September 2018, available at https://verfassungsblog.de/the-diciotti-affair-beyond-the-populist-farce/ (accessed on 7 October 2018).

Salvadego, Laura, "I respingimenti sommari di migranti alle frontiere terrestri dell'enclave di Melilla", in *Diritti umani e diritto internazionale*, Vol. 12, N. 1, 2018, p. 199 ff.

Sapienza, Rosario, "Art. 1", in *Commentario breve alla Convenzione europea* (S. Bartole, P. De Sena, V. Zagrebelsky eds), Padova, Cedam, 2012, p. 13 ff.

Scheinin, Martin, "Extraterritorial Effect of the International Covenant on Civil and Political Rights", in *Extraterritorial Application of Human Rights Treaties* (F. Coomans, T. Kamminga eds), Antwerp, Intersentia, 2004, p. 73 ff.

Scholten, Sophie, Minderhoud, Paul, "Regulating Immigration Control: Carrier Sanctions in the Netherlands", in *European Journal of Migration and Law*, Vol. 10, N. 2, 2008, p. 123 ff.

Scovazzi, Tullio, "Human Rights and Immigration at Sea", in *Human Rights and Immigration* (Ruth Rubio-Marín ed.), Oxford, Oxford University Press, 2014, p. 212 ff.

Scovazzi, Tullio, "Il respingimento di un dramma umano collettivo e le sue conseguenze", in *L'immigrazione irregolare via mare nella giurisprudenza italiana e nell'esperienza europea* (A. Antonucci, I. Papanicolopulu, T. Scovazzi eds), Torino, G. Giappichelli Editore, 2016, p. 45 ff.

Scovazzi, Tulllio, "Some Legal Questions Relating to Irregular Migrants at Sea", in *Migration in the Mediterranean Area and the Challenges for Hosting European Society* (G. Cataldi, M. Pace, A. Liguori eds), Napoli, Editoriale scientifica, 2017, p. 179 ff.

Scovazzi, Tullio, "Some Cases in the Italian Practice Relating to Illegal Migration at Sea" in *International Law and the Protection of Humanity* (P. Acconci, D.D. Cattin, A. Marchesi, G. Palmisano V. Santori eds.), Leiden, Brill Nijhoff, 2016, p. 196 ff.

Seibert-Fohr, Anja, "The ICJ Judgment in the Bosnian Genocide Case and Beyond: A Need to Reconceptualise", 20 February 2009, available at https://papers.ssrn.com/sol3/papers.cfm?abstract_id=1342817 (accessed on 7 October 2018).

Seibert-Fohr, Anja, "From Complicity to Due Diligence: When Do States Incur Responsibility for Their Involvement in Serious International

Wrongdoing?", in *German Yearbook of International Law*, Vol. 60, N. 2017, 2018, p. 668 ff.

Simma, Bruno, "From Bilateralism to Community Interest in International Law", in *Recueil des Cours de l'Académie de Droit International*, Leiden/ Boston, Martinus Nijhoff Publishers, Vol. 250, 1994, p. 217 ff.

Spinedi, Marina, Gianelli, Alessandra, Alaimo, Maria Luisa (eds), *La codificazione della responsabilità internazionale degli Stati alla prova dei fatti. Problemi e spunti di riflessione*, Milano, Giuffrè, 2006.

Skogly Sigrun, Gibney Mark, "Transnational Human Rights Obligations", in *Human Rights Quarterly*, Vol. 24, N. 3, 2002, p. 781 ff.

Skogly, Sigrun, *Beyond National Borders: States' Human Rights Obligations in International Cooperation*, Antwerpen-Oxford, Intersentia, March 2006.

Skordas, Achilles, "A 'Blind Spot' in the Migration Debate? International Responsibility of the EU and Its Member States for Cooperating with the Libyan Coastguard and Militias", in *EU Immigration and Asylum Law and Policy*, 30 January 2018, available at http://eumigrationlawblog.eu/a-blind-spot-in-the-migration-debate-international-responsibility-of-the-eu-and-its-member-states-for-cooperating-with-the-libyan-coastguard-and-militias/ (accessed on 7 October 2018).

Spagnolo, Andrea, "Di intese segrete e alibi parlamentari: tra la decisione del Tar sull'accordo col Niger e il Global Compact sulle migrazioni", *SidiBlog*, 5 December 2018, available at http://www.sidiblog.org/2018/12/05/di-intese-segrete-e-alibi-parlamentari-tra-la-decisione-del-tar-sullaccordo-col-niger-e-il-global-compact-sulle-migrazioni/ (accessed on 5 December 2018).

Spijkerboer, Thomas, "Human Costs of Border Control", in *European Journal of Migration and Law*, 2007, p. 127 ff., available at http://thomasspijkerboer. eu/wp-content/uploads/2014/12/The-Human-Costs-of-Border-Control3. pdf (accessed on 7 October 2018).

Spijkerboer, Thomas, "Bifurcation of People, Bifurcation of Law: Externalization of Migration Policy before the EU Court of Justice", in *Journal of Refugee Studies*, Vol. 31, N. 2, June 2018, p. 216 ff.

Strik, Tineke, "The Global Approach to Migration and Mobility", in *Groningen Journal of International Law*, Vol. 5, N. 2, 2017, p. 310 ff.

Talmon, Stefan, "A Plurality of Responsible Actors: International Responsibility for Acts of the Coalition Provisional Authority in Iraq", in *The Iraq War and International Law* (P. Shiner A. Williams eds), Oxford, Hart Publishing, 2008, p. 185 ff.

Tan, Nikolas Feith, "State Responsibility for International Cooperation on Migration Control: The Case of Australia", in *Oxford Monitor If Forced Migration*, Vol. 5, N. 2, 2015, p. 8 ff., available at http://oxmofm.com/ wp-content/uploads/2015/12/NIKOLAS-FEITH-TAN-State-responsibility-for-international-cooperation-on-migration-control2.pdf (accessed on 7 October 2018).

Tan, Nikolas Feith, "State Responsibility and Migration Control: Australia's International Deterrence Model", in *Human Rights and the Dark Side of*

Globalisation (T. Gammeltoft-Hansen, J. Vedsted-Hansen, eds), London/ New York, Routledge, 2017, p. 215 ff.

Thym, Daniel, "Why the EU-Turkey Deal is Legal and a Step in the Right Direction" in *Verfassungsblog*, 9 March 2016, available at https://verfassungs blog.de/why-the-eu-turkey-deal-is-legal-and-a-step-in-the-right-direction/ (accessed on 7 October 2018).

Trevisanut, Seline "The Principle of Non-Refoulement at Sea and the Effectiveness of Asylum Protection", in *Max Planck Yearbook of United Nations Law*, Vol. 12, 2008, pp. 205 ff.

Trevisanut, Seline, *Immigrazione irregolare via mare. Diritto internazionale e diritto dell'Unione europea*, Napoli, Jovene Editore, 2012.

Tzevelekos, Vassilis, "Reconstructing the Effective Control Criterion in Extraterritorial Human Rights Breaches: Direct Attribution of Wrongfulness, Due Diligence, and Concurrent Responsibility", *Michigan Journal of International Law*, Vol. 36, N. 1, 2014, p. 129 ff.

Tzevelekos, Vassilis P., Katselli Proukaki, Elena, "Migrants at Sea: A Duty of Plural States to Protect (Extraterritorially)?", in *Nordic Journal of International Law*, Vol. 86, N. 4, 2017, p. 427 ff.

Van Berlo, Patrick, "The Protection of Asylum Seekers in Australian-Pacific Offshore Processing: The Legal Deficit of Human Rights in a Nodal Reality", in *Human Rights Law Review*, 2017, p. 33 ff., available at https://academic. oup.com/hrlr/article/17/1/33/2525422 (accessed on 30 November 2018).

Van Malleghem, *Pieter-Augustijn*, "C.J.U.E., Aff. jointes C-208/17 P à C-210/17 P, ordonnance du 12 septembre 2018, NF, NG et NM, ECLI:EU:C:2018:705", in *Centre Charles De Visscher pour le droit international et européen*, 4 October 2018, available at https://uclouvain.be/fr/instituts-recherche/juri/cedie/ actualites/c-j-u-e-aff-jointes-c-208-17-p-a-c-210-17-p-ordonnance-du-12-septembre-2018-nf-ng-et-nm.html#_ftn17 (accessed on 30 October 2018).

Vassallo Paleologo, Fulvio, "Elementi per un esposto nei confronti del governo italiano a seguito dell'applicazione del Memorandum d'intesa sottoscritto con il governo di Tripoli il 2 febbraio 2017", 14 June 2017, available at: https://www.a-dif.org/2017/06/14/elementi-per-un-esposto-nei-confronti-del-governo-italiano-a-seguito-dellapplicazione-del-memorandum-dintesa-sottoscritto-con-il-governo-di-tripoli-il-2-febbraio-2017 (accessed on 7 October 2018).

Vavoula, Niovi, "Of Carrots and Sticks: A Punitive Shift in the Reform of the Visa Code", in *EU Immigration and Asylum Law and Policy*, 5 September 2018, available at http://eumigrationlawblog.eu/of-carrots-and-sticks-a-punitive-shift-in-the-reform-of-the-visa-code (accessed on 30 October 2018).

Vitiello, Daniela, "L'azione esterna dell'Unione europea in materia di immigrazione e asilo: linee di tendenza e proposte per il futuro", in *Diritto, Immigrazione e Cittadinanza*, Vol. XVIII, N. 3–4, 2016, p. 9 ff.

Vitiello, Daniela, "Il contributo dell'Unione europea alla governance internazionale dei flussi di massa di rifugiati e migranti: spunti per una rilettura critica dei Global Compacts", in *Diritto, Immigrazione e Cittadinanza*, N. 3,

2018, p. 1 ff., available at https://www.dirittoimmigrazionecittadinanza.it/ saggi/304-saggio-vitiello/file (accessed on 3 November 2018).

Vitiello, Daniela, "Il diritto di cercare asilo ai tempi dell'Aquarius", in *SIDI-Blog*, 29 June 2018, available at http://www.sidiblog.org/2018/06/29/il-diritto-di-cercare-asilo-ai-tempi-dellaquarius/ (accessed on 7 October 2018).

Wilde, Ralph, "Legal "Black Hole"?: Extraterritorial State Action and International Treaty Law on Civil and Political Rights", in *Michigan Journal of International Law*, Vol. 26, N. 3, 2005, p. 739 ff, available at https://repository.law.umich.edu/cgi/viewcontent.cgi?article=1235&context=mjil (accessed on 7 October 2018).

Xenos, Dimitris, *The Positive Obligations of the State under the European Convention If Human Rights*, London/ New York, Routledge, 2012.

Zaiotti, Ruben (ed.), *Externalizing Migration Management. Europe, North America and the Spread of 'Remote Control' Practices*, London, Routledge, 2016.

Ziebritzki, Catharina, Nestler, Robert, "Implementation of the EU-Turkey Statement: EU Hotspots and Restriction of Asylum Seekers' Freedom of Movement", in *EU Immigration and Asylum Law and Policy*, 22 June 2018, available at http://eumigrationlawblog.eu/implementation-of-the-eu-turkey-statement-eu-hotspots-and-restriction-of-asylum-seekers-freedom-of-movement/ (accessed on 5 December 2018).

Index

Printed in the United States
by Baker & Taylor Publisher Services